Young AND Mighty

Every owner of a physical copy of this edition of

YOUNG AND MIGHTY

can download the eBook for free direct from us at Harriman House, in a DRM-free format that can be read on any eReader, tablet or smartphone.

Simply head to:

ebooks.harriman-house.com/youngandmighty

to get your copy now.

Hh
Young
AND
Mighty
Your SECRET WEAPON for earning some money, changing the world, and spending your future doing what you love
HENRY PATTERSON
(AGED 14)

HARRIMAN HOUSE LTD

18 College Street

Petersfield

Hampshire

GU31 4AD

GREAT BRITAIN

Tel: +44 (0)1730 233870

Email: enquiries@harriman-house.com

Website: www.harriman-house.com

First published in 2018.

Illustrations by Becky Down
Cover author photo by CO Photography

Paperback ISBN: 978-0-85719-657-6
eBook ISBN: 978-0-85719-658-3

British Library Cataloguing in Publication Data
A CIP catalogue record for this book can be obtained from the British Library.

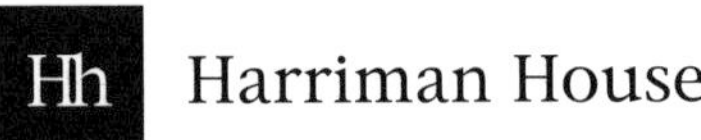

{CONTENTS}

{ ABOUT THE AUTHOR }

Henry Patterson set up his first business selling manure at the age of four and hasn't looked back. Despite not always fitting in at school, Henry has taken his own path based on the principle that whatever you do should make you and others happy.

Henry frequently speaks to audiences of young people all over the world to share his ideas about business and about the importance of making your own way in life.

In January 2018, now 14, Henry set up Young & Mighty, an online space to inspire young people to turn their idea into a thing.

★ **youngmighty.com**

★ **@henryjpatterson** (Instagram)

Preface

WHO I AM

Hello! My name is Henry Patterson and I'm 14 years old.

When I was four, I started to earn money selling manure. Then, when I was nine, I wrote a storybook about a mouse and an owl and started my own business, called Not Before Tea, selling products based on the characters.

Since then, I've been lucky enough to follow my interests in business and music, and I regularly talk to young people (and older ones) about how to find your own way in life and do the things you love.

This book includes my tips on how to make a bit of extra money when you're young, for you or for a good cause. But it's also about doing whatever makes you happy.

WHY I WROTE THIS BOOK

A few years ago I was named 'One to Watch' in the Great British Entrepreneur Awards. One of my prizes was a book voucher and I really wanted to get a book that would give me tips and tricks for being a successful entrepreneur – an inspiring read, something I could follow over the next few years and really learn from.

As I browsed the bookshop I slowly discovered that there were no fun, creative business books. I ended up buying a journal instead. Over the next few years of running my business, making mistakes, learning from them and chatting to amazing entrepreneurs like Sir Richard Branson, I kept writing in that  journal. That journal is now this book.

I wanted to show that anyone can turn their passion into more than just a hobby. I turned my little sweet stall into a business and this allowed me to meet fantastic people and travel the world.

You don't need to be ridiculously wealthy, cool or good-looking to run a business, or be a vlogger or a celebrity to make a difference.

Just look at me: a bit chubby, with a stammer, messy hair and very odd teeth.

Anyone can do it and this book will show you how.

HOW TO USE THIS BOOK

The good news is that this book is not something you need to read from start to finish, though it would be nice if you did. You certainly don't have to read it in order.

I have divided it into five parts:

★ **Part One** contains lots of ideas on how to earn a bit of money *right now*. Many of the ideas are something you can just do for a short time and then stop. If you have seen a pair of trainers you want, pick an idea and hopefully it will enable you to make the money you need.

★ **Part Two** is all about fundraising. Life is not just about getting stuff for yourself but helping others too. There are lots of ideas here for how to raise money for any cause close to your heart (and have great fun along the way).

★ **Part Three** is a complete guide to getting your own business off the ground. This could just be taking one of the ideas from Part One to the next level – but perhaps you want to develop a bigger idea. In this section I have teamed up with some experts for advice on finance, structure, legal stuff, marketing and how to get yourself featured in the media.

★ **Part Four** is for you to get creative. It's full of planners and thought-provoking pages for you to get stuck into.

★ **Part Five** is all about learning from the best. I have interviewed the top people in their professions to give you (and me!) advice. Knowing what they know now, what would they tell their younger selves? I was once told it's great to learn from your mistakes but even better to learn from other people's.

Use and abuse this book: underline things, circle bits to remember, turn down corners and scribble on every page.

It is your book, your secret weapon to make sure you end up filling your future with things you love doing.

Oh, and don't forget to keep in touch along the way.

Henry X

My Story

Christmas Day, 2013. My stammer had got so bad that it had just taken me over a minute to thank my grandma for my presents. As my mother said goodnight to me that evening, I burst into tears. I could not carry on like this; I wanted to get my voice back.

It was a turning point in my life and the reason that, at 14 years old, I have set up, run and sold a business.

LOSING MY VOICE

I was born in Northampton on 15 January 2004. I was the first furless child in a huge family of dogs, horses, sheep, goats, hens, ducks, cats and a faithful Labrador named Bert. We all lived at a riding school in Holcot, Northamptonshire.

I have been told I was an excellent baby who was asleep every single night by 6.30 pm and gave my parents no problems at all. I went to nursery very early as my mother worked and I loved every single minute. I did not progress in a conventional way. My first word was 'believe'. I was standing super early but walking really late, reading really early but writing did not come as easily, and I was the last in my group to come out of nappies.

As a toddler, I hated swings and roundabouts, could not ride a bike (and still can't) and was pretty terrible at anything to do with sport.

The one thing I *did* love, however, was music. It was through music that my parents started to realise that I looked at the world slightly differently to other children. I just had to listen to a song once to be able to memorise the melody and lyrics.

At the age of four we moved to Buckinghamshire and I left my beloved nursery, which threw me into turmoil for a few months.

I started at the village school early and was very proud of my uniform. I had a mass of blonde curls and looked quite the angel. Unfortunately I was turning into quite the little terror. I simply could not tolerate people who did not inspire and challenge me.

I wanted to talk about antiques and how the earth was created, not count the sides of a square. Six months in, I was asked to leave.

My mother got a call one lunchtime asking if she could come and collect me within the hour because I was not ready for school.

Social services were called as I had been expelled from mainstream school and they diagnosed me as a healthy, happy boy, with a huge appetite to learn. I had a trial day at a school in Buckingham which had a work/play/work/play ethic.

I instantly bonded with the headmaster, who was an explorer and had a drawer of fossils and rocks. He was one of the few that instantly got me but also told my mother that we were in for a bumpy ride over the next few years. He was not wrong.

I got off to a great start at my new school and started to make friends. However, I found it hard to rein in my enthusiasm and one day my mother was asked for "a word" when she came to pick me up. She was then asked for a word the following week – and the week after that.

It was never anything serious. I just irritated my teachers with constant questions and opinions. It was my curiosity that made me start my first venture. I was in a garden centre with my parents and I saw a sign saying 'Horse manure, £3'. I remembered my father complaining that the farmer was charging £200 to take away manure from our stables. I asked why we were paying to get it removed and not selling it. After being told that it was quite time-consuming to bag it up, I asked if I could sell it. I was told that I was allowed to but had to make the bags and the sign; it was my own business. I filled one bag and then got some help with the other two as it was very hard going. I put three bags outside our house and made a sign. I must have thought it was called "myor" because that's how I wrote it on my sign.

An hour later, someone drove past and bought all three bags. I had £1.50 and was delighted. I decided to stop the business as I had made my fortune and was shattered from making up the bags. However, I still remember the sense of achievement as I squeezed my fingers around the two coins I had earned.

School was not going as well. I started not to get invited to parties and was rarely invited to tea. I was branded 'the naughty one' and I think my mother was affected by this exclusion more than me.

Despite all this, I loved the social side of the playground. We all started to bring in little plastic figures to play with and soon started to swap our spares to build up our collections. Because this could take a long time, I suggested that we could also buy figures we wanted from each other, which meant that the children had to bring money into school, which was forbidden.

The headmistress (we had two head teachers) heard about this and my mother and I were called to her office. I was given the usual ticking off and was told that my trading had to stop. I remember walking out of the room, furious, when I suddenly had a great idea to get round the problem. I turned to the headmistress and asked: "How about PayPal?"

Needless to say the business never traded again. I have learned from this, however: always offer your customers more than one way to pay.

I also developed a love of writing stories and took great pleasure in writing scripts for my friends to perform at playtime. Everything I did had to be an official event. I recall making all my friends join my playtime drama club before they could be cast with a part.

The club was called Break Free and the first play was centred around a group of children who met some unicorns and flew off over the school gates to see the world.

Even this harmless club was brought to an abrupt halt when the mother of my friend found a membership card in his blazer. The next day a child safety officer was brought into the school and we all had a lesson on why we should never leave the school grounds, even on a unicorn. Looking back, I guess I can see why this was taken so seriously. But it was always me in the firing line.

I continued to challenge the school system and my teacher had a meeting with my parents to suggest that I see an educational psychologist to get advice on whether I needed extra support. After a few sessions with her it appeared that I had a very high IQ and after some trips to the child behaviour unit at Bedford I was diagnosed with Asperger syndrome. It was mild and this label has never really been used since. But it helped my parents understand why I approached everything in a slightly different way.

From day one, I hated games lessons. I hated the loud changing room, I hated the whistle and I was very slow at getting dressed and undressed. I've always struggled with coordination and it was at this time I was diagnosed with dyspraxia.

My games teacher, who from now on I am going to call Mr Shorts, took an instant dislike to me. On the days where I was really slow at getting changed, I was told that I had to miss my break and get dressed and undressed in my games kit six times. The changing room was so frightening when I was on my own. I hate being on my own. I got anxious and found this made me even slower.

However, this was nothing compared to wearing a mouth guard. I have a very sensitive reflux and found that I simply could not keep the mouth guard in my mouth without gagging. We went to the dentist to get a special one made but it was just as bad. Mr Shorts said I had to wear it and get on with it.

The issue with changing and the mouth guard started to dominate my life. I dreaded daily games. I found that my anxiety in the lessons before games did not help my concentration. I was constantly told that I was not applying myself. Once again my parents were called in on a regular basis to be told that I was holding up the lessons. In fact, they were called in so often they never attended a parents' evening until I was 11 as they were kept updated on a daily basis.

My music class kept me going. I had such a wonderful teacher who knew exactly how to inspire me. He was the only one who ever praised me and he even accepted me in the chapel choir, which was such an honour. I was one of 16 members. I wore my robe with such pride and I respected him so much for giving me the opportunity. He was eccentric, jolly and the most amazing pianist but very, very strict. I would never dare to misbehave.

I applied to join a summer holiday choral course, which needed a reference from my school choirmaster. He must have said nice things, because I got in. I am eternally grateful for this, as the choral course has been a vital part of my life to this day. When I was singing I could be myself. It became my safe place and my wonderful choirmaster became my friend.

The world came crashing down when I returned to school and learnt that my music teacher had suddenly become ill and died.

To this day he is in my thoughts whenever I sing or have an audition. My wonderful headmaster retired that year, too, and I was alone in a school where no one understood me.

I was constantly told I was useless. My mother was frequently called in and told that I was not fitting in and that it was a shame I was not more like the other children. I only found out recently that she would cry on the way home from school pretty much every day.

Games continued to be unbearable and I started to develop a stammer. Very quickly it prevented me from saying a sentence. I saw a speech therapist who said it was an anxiety issue.

Christmas arrived and it was so bad I could hardly talk.

That night I burst into tears as games and Mr Shorts were only getting worse. I couldn't keep letting this ruin my week, my holidays, and now Christmas. I took a deep breath and said the words I never wanted to say: "I want to leave my school." My parents had been talking about me changing school for a while now and I had begged them to let me stay as there was so much I loved about it. But there was also so much that I hated.

This was the first big decision I ever had to make – and in business, making decisions is something you have to do often. So, in some  ways I thank Mr Shorts for giving me a reason to make a decision like that. I left the following Easter.

I took six months off school as my parents didn't want me to start a new school with such a terrible stammer. They wanted to try to get to the root of my issues and find out what would really keep me inspired and focused.

FINDING MY VOICE

So here I was, not at school, with a terrible stammer, wondering if I would ever be myself again.

My mum noticed how lost I was feeling and said we needed a project. I had been messing around with creating crazy mixes with sweets like chocolate raisins and jelly worms. In my head, they were sold in a sweet shop which was run by a mouse and an owl.

I ended up with six jars of sweets and started selling them to family and friends. I decided that I wanted to go further and sell my products to the public, but I had no idea where to start. I asked my mother because she has always worked in marketing. After a long conversation she taught me how to write a press release, which we sent off that night.

Two days later it was picked up by the *Daily Mail* and I was thrilled! That day we got 62,000 hits on our website.

As much as I loved all of this, there was a downside. I went online and saw horrible comments about me from the public on news sites. It was heartbreaking. I had a simple choice: keep going and get past it, or give up and stop it. I loved what I was doing and chose option one.

I learnt a lesson that day. If you really love what you do, no one can tell you that you can't do it.

The next two weeks were a blur. It seemed as though I spent my life being interviewed. I loved every moment of it. In one interview with the *Huffington Post* the man on the other end of the phone said: "So, Henry, I suppose you're going to write a book about this then?"

That night I sat down and began work on a storybook. I thought of eight characters: Pip the Mouse, Sherb the Owl, Vera Vole, Martha Mole, Billy the Cat, Brendan Badger, Mr Fox and Bubbles the Goldfish. They lived in a sweet shop run by Mrs Pinny. The shop was called Not Before Tea because that's what grown-ups say when you ask for sweets! The two main characters were Sherb and Pip, so I titled the book *The Adventures of Sherb and Pip*.

I guess it never occurred to me that lots of people read these articles. I started getting invitations and opportunities to some very exciting places.

One day, I got an invitation to the Great British Entrepreneur Awards, which was amazing. It really was the first time I'd felt proud in a long time. I won the 'One to Watch' award and was overjoyed. I cried my eyes out on the way home as I didn't want it to end.

So much had come out of those past few weeks and they truly were the best few weeks of my life. Only a couple of days later the head buyer from Bentalls (a big department store) wanted to meet me. A week later our products were on their shelves.

This was only the beginning. After those ten years of not fitting in, my life had changed forever.

A year later Not Before Tea opened its first shop in Buckinghamshire, selling jars of sweets and children's wash bags and pencil cases featuring the characters from my book. My mother gave up her job in marketing and took care of running my business while I was at school.

It was lovely to bring the shop I had imagined in the storybook to life. We only took the lease for one year, so it was important we learnt what customers liked, what looked good on the shelves and how to display our products.

During this time, we managed to get over 70 other shops to stock our products. I tried to visit as many as I could and spent most of my Saturdays doing storytime sessions and book signings.

I was making a little money. But I soon realised that all the money earned by a young business needs to be invested back into it, to allow it to grow. I was given a small amount after the success of the book and I'm proud to say that I'm sitting right next to my profits now – my adorable little pug, Martha.

In September 2014, I joined a new school that suited me better.

On my second week, I came home from school and my mother said that she had some exciting news. She said that *The One Show* had invited me on with Sir Richard Branson… next Monday. I can't really remember if I was crying or smiling, so let's just say I was smying or criling.

The day arrived and I remember so clearly stepping out of the black taxi and just looking up at the magnificent BBC building in Portland Place, London. Me being me, I got lost and almost walked into Radio 1 instead.

When we finally found the studio it was even better than I thought it would be. The lights, the cameras, the sense of excitement. It was exactly what any ten-year-old would think of when someone said 'TV studio'.

My big moment came. I looked Sir Richard Branson in the eye with two of Britain's most well-known television presenters either side of him and asked my question. "What can I do to help grow my business?"

His mouth opened and I'll never forget the words of wisdom that Sir Richard uttered. He said:

> "First of all, promise me that you won't go into the airline or train business."

I must admit – though it wasn't the exact answer I was looking for – it made my day.

Sir Richard did give me some great tips after this, and to this day I carry a notebook around with me at all times in order to write down advice and ideas.

After *The One Show* I was invited to speak at a conference called Mumpreneur (or, according to spellcheck, the 'murderer' conference). I gave a talk and discovered that I had a passion for public speaking.

Little did I know that, one year later, in March 2016, I would be speaking at Retail Week Live at the O2.

Around January someone else appeared in my life, not in person – though that is at the top of my bucket list – but through music. I discovered the genius Lin-Manuel Miranda. Lin has written two musicals. One called *In the Heights*, a musical which you can't not dance to. And another called *Hamilton*. It would be a total understatement if I said that *Hamilton* changed my life. It still inspires me every day.

Another year on, here I am, just turned 14 and so excited about what lies ahead.

Four years ago my stammer was so bad I couldn't string a sentence together. Since then, I have spoken on stage to huge audiences around the world.

Four years ago my teachers would constantly tell me how useless I was and asked why I couldn't be like the rest of the class. Today I have received hundreds of letters from people telling me how much I have inspired them.

And four years ago I couldn't sleep for fear of what the next day would bring. Tonight I will fall into bed with exhaustion from the excitement of the day, and dream of the opportunities tomorrow will bring.

When you feel like you are in a really lonely dark place, open your eyes and look for light. You won't have to wait long until you find it... no matter how small the ray.

PART ONE: 30 Ways to Earn Some Money

This part of the book is all about quick, clever or creative ways you can earn some money – things that you can do straight away, without having to set up a business or worry about the long term.

I have done a number of them personally. I have spoken to other young people who have done the rest. They can be a great way to get a feel for the kind of business you might one day want to create. Or they can just be a great way to make a bit of cash to buy something you want!

Don't forget to also have a look in Part Five for inspiration – one of the questions I've asked everyone I've met is how they would try and double £10 in five days. The answers may surprise (and inspire) you!

A QUICK OFFICIAL BIT

This part of the book is full of ways to make extra pocket money. Because of our age, we need the permission of parents or guardians to do most of the things I have suggested.

The best thing to do is to choose one of the ideas, sit down with whoever looks after you, and get their advice on how best to do it.

Many online marketplaces require someone over the age of 18 to set up the selling account and link it to their bank account.

If you are advertising a service you will need a phone number or email address. Hopefully your parents/guardians can manage this side of the business and take the bookings for you. *You must not give out your phone number or go to people's homes if you don't know them, even if it is about work.* It is just too dangerous.

Your parents/guardians will probably want to come along the first few times you work for a customer, just to check you are OK. This is fine. Please don't think that your customers will worry you are not capable of doing the job just because someone older has come along with you.

My mother comes to all my events and conferences. To be honest, I wouldn't want to go on my own. I feel safer with her tagging along and I need her to help me with phone calls and the financial side of things anyway.

Think of your parents/guardians as part of your team rather than someone just keeping an eye on you.

Now let's get down to choosing you a fun and quick way to earn some money...

WAYS TO EARN MONEY OUTDOORS

1. CAR WASHING

Car washing is one of my favourite ways to earn some money. I look out of the window and see so many dirty cars everywhere. But I don't *just* see dirty cars, I see a great opportunity. The best part is, car washing will cost you almost nothing to set up and run.

Fill a bucket with hot water and washing-up liquid, buy a sponge and you've got your equipment sorted.

One of the most important things is advertising your service well. There are so many car washers out there and it can sometimes be hard to stand out from the crowd.

You'll need some leaflets and posters. Check out the quick section at the end of Part One – 'How to spread the word!' on page 57 – for how to do that really well.

You could be mobile and visit people's driveways or set up in a local car park.

My local car-washing company gives customers a little air freshener with every clean, which is a lovely touch. You can buy packs of five from your local supermarket quite cheaply. It is extra touches like this that will make people return to you. Remember to take account of the cost of this in your price, though.

Pricing can be tricky – but because you have low costs, you can afford to be competitive. Think about how much money you would be happy to earn in one hour, then work out how many cars you can wash in that time. If you want £10 per hour and you can wash three cars in that time, I would charge £4 a car. This gives you a bit extra for a new sponge every now and then (and an air freshener or two).

Don't forget to leave a business card with drivers so they can call you again to re-book.

What you need to do this job:

★ Bucket

★ Sponge

★ Cloth for drying

★ Washing-up liquid

★ Supply of water

2. DOG WALKING

Dog walking is a great way to earn some money. It can mean a lot to those who are busy in the morning because they have to go to work, or are ill and struggling to walk their dog.

Dog walking is a big responsibility. You also need to love being around dogs. That is probably the most important thing.

You also need to make sure that you understand that people are paying you to walk their dog *in all conditions*. It may be boiling hot or freezing cold, sunny or snowy, rainy or windy – the dogs still need their walk.

You will also need to sit down with an adult, plan your route and time it.

You need to keep the route consistent so that an adult will know where you are at all times. Make yourself familiar with the walk so that you don't get lost.

After you've planned everything, it's time to let your local area know about your new service.

leaflet and poster time! Check the quick section at the end of Part One – 'How to spread the word!' on page 57 – for some advice on creating posters and flyers.

You can either charge per walk, by the distance you are walking or per dog. Maybe you can walk a few dogs at the same time – as long as they are all friends.

What you need to do this job:

★ Good walking shoes

★ Warm clothes in the winter

3. A PITCH AT A CAR-BOOT SALE

Selling at a car-boot sale is my number one tip for earning some money. The beauty of a car-boot sale is not only do you get great experience but you can sell pretty much anything. Whether DVDs, computer games, books, clothes or toys you will learn everything you need to know about selling a product. It's actually great experience for running your own business too.

To be honest, there is no right or wrong way to sell at a car-boot sale. It's all about trial and error (trust me, I made some errors!).

Make sure you go with a good quantity of things to sell (stock) and a clear vision of what your stall is going to look like.

The first thing you need to do is work out what you are going to sell. The simple answer is anything you no longer need. You can ask your family too. Even ask your friends if they have things to sell. You could team up, run a stall together and share the profits.

I would draw a sketch of how you want to lay out your stall, then when you get there you can spend less time planning and more time making it look great.

When customers buy a product it's because it looks really amazing and because they feel they need it in their life. Most of the time the display sells it to them.

Think of it like this. There's a great new phone that's just been released and two different shops decide that they want to stock it and each shop has identical pricing and identical packaging.

The first shop has stacked all the boxes on top of each other with a badly written sign saying 'New Phone'. The second shop has a polished display case with stunning lighting and a beautifully printed sign reading 'The Phone of the Year'. Of course, we all buy from the second one.

Once you've planned your stall you need to price your items. A mistake I made when I went to a car-boot sale was pricing. I didn't plan anything. So when I got there I had two things that I had to do: design the stall and price all of my items.

That wasn't great!

Go to your nearest supermarket and buy yourself some price tags. The day before you go to your boot sale, price all your items to save you the trouble of doing it when you get there.

You're almost there. When you arrive at the boot sale you will probably see a person wearing a high-vis jacket ushering cars into the venue. These are the people you want to speak to about your pitch. Once you've spoken to them, get set up and start selling.

There are just a few tips about selling. The first is simple. Smile. Remember, these people are offering to give you money. Be friendly, say hello, ask them how their day is going. If they're looking at a product, maybe explain a bit about it. Customers love to feel as though they're wanted, as if they're part of the experience.

The second is a bit trickier. Occasionally a customer may ask you for a discount. You need to remember, there is nothing wrong with this. They are not trying to catch you out, just get a bargain. Another thing to remember is that this is your stand and only you can make the final decision.

Don't be afraid to say no if you feel someone is asking for too low a price but always stay open-minded and try to bargain. At the end of the day you won't want to take lots of items home.

Make sure you write down everything you sell and the price of each item. Before you go home, add up your total and take away all the money that you've spent (price tags and the cost of your pitch). Whatever is left is your profit.

What you need to do this job:

★ Products (stock)

★ Price tags/labels

- ★ Pen

- ★ Notebook

- ★ Food and drink (to keep you going throughout the day)

- ★ Blanket or tablecloth

- ★ Chair

- ★ Change (called 'petty cash')

- ★ Money belt

4. PAPER ROUND

A paper round is one of the most traditional ways for young people to earn some extra money.

The first thing you need to think about is transport. The classic 'paper-round-mobile' is the bike, but you may not have a bike. You could use a scooter, skateboard or just your feet. Anything to help you get around.

This next bit can be a bit off-putting, especially if, like me, you're not a morning person. People like their papers in time for breakfast so you'll have to get up early. A bit like dog walking, you also have to do this in all weather conditions.

Your first step is to go to a newsagent and ask if they need someone. Make sure you ask a few newsagents to see who offers the best rate. When you go in, make sure you're friendly.

Like all job interviews, you are potentially looking at someone who is willing to pay you. Maybe even say what you are saving up for. I would say something like this: "Hello, I'm Henry. I live just down the road. I'm saving up for a dog and was wondering if you needed any help delivering papers?" Something along those lines.

If they say yes, that's great. They'll give you a start date and a rate for the work and off you go.

You also need to know your route really well. I would find a map of your village or street, circle all of the houses that you're delivering to, and find the fastest, safest route.

Before you leave the house, make sure you eat and drink something to give you enough energy. Wear the right clothes for the time of year and carry anything you need to keep you safe (like a torch and high-vis vest if you're working in the dark). You may also want to carry a phone for emergencies. If you don't have a phone, perhaps your parents will lend you one.

You'll get the hang of it very quickly and soon notice your hard work paying off.

What you need to do this job:

★ Good alarm clock

★ Warm clothes and gloves in the winter

★ Torch and high-vis vest if it's dark

★ Phone for emergencies

5. GARDENING

If you love gardening, it can be a fantastic way to earn a bit of money. It involves being outdoors, getting dirty and (not to state the obvious) gardening.

If you are super knowledgeable about plants and flowers that is great, but this job could equally suit someone who is just hardworking and can mow the lawn, sweep leaves, pull up weeds and do general tidying.

Posters and leaflets will be crucial for getting the word out. *Check the quick section at the end of Part One – 'How to spread the word!' on page 57 – for how to do that effectively.*

For gardening, the essentials are: Your service – gardening. What type of gardening you do, like cutting grass, planting seeds, pruning trees, sweeping paths, weeding, watering. Your hourly rate and what days and times you're available. Lastly, a contact number/email.

I can't really give you advice on the actual gardening other than don't crash the lawnmower into a wall. (I don't know anything about gardening.) All I can say is that these people are paying you to do something that you enjoy. Make the most of it. (If you don't enjoy it and it feels like a burden then why on earth are you even bothering?) Being outside can be really therapeutic. Our local gardener listens to his iPod as he gardens and can often be seen dancing away on the lawn.

What you need to do this job:

★ Gardening gloves

★ Overalls or old clothes

If you don't have any gardening tools, explain this to your customers at the start – you may be able to use theirs.

6. ODD JOBS

Doing odd jobs around someone's property can really help you earn some money.

Whether it's in a garden shed or in Buckingham Palace, there's always something that someone needs doing.

First, think about the equipment you have and the services you can offer.

Some ideas are: fence painting, jet washing, cleaning patio furniture, scrubbing doorsteps, raking gravel, collecting leaves, shovelling snow, polishing shoes and watering plants.

Poster and leaflet time. Check the quick section at the end of Part One – 'How to spread the word!' on page 57 – for how to get that sorted properly.

Remember, health and safety are really important. Be sensible and don't do anything that's outside your comfort zone.

What you need to do this job:

★ It depends on what odd jobs you are willing to do

7. PLANT SELLING

Selling plants is a slow way to make a bit of money but it's 100% free. You need no money to get going. Which is brilliant.

To start, collect some seeds from flowers, vegetables or fruit.

You can also take a cutting from a plant. To do this, cut a stem from the plant – don't just tear it off. Put the stem in a pot of soil and keep watering it. It will start to root and grow in a few weeks.

By the way, don't just go into people's gardens and chop bits off their plants. I am sure if you ask your family and neighbours they will have lots of different plants that you could take cuttings from.

You don't have to buy pots. You can use yoghurt cartons, margarine tubs or jam jars.

Once your plants have grown, you can sell them.

When I was selling manure back in 2008, I simply sold it outside my front gate with a sign saying 'leave 50p in the post box'. You could do that (though there is always a risk that some nasty person could come and steal your hard-earned money and plants – it's perhaps a bit more appealing than shoplifting dung). You could also go to a car-boot sale or a market. Either way, you've got some planting to do first.

What you need to do this job:

★ A garden, a corner of a kitchen, or just a windowsill

★ Access to plants (for cuttings) or fruit seeds

★ Soil

★ Water

8. BIKE REPAIRS

This certainly isn't my strong point as I can't even ride a bike let alone fix one, but bike repairs is a handy job and another brilliant way to earn some money.

Let's say that in some fantasy miracle world I somehow knew how to ride a bike, I would probably break it in my first day. I would need to find someone who is the opposite of me and who is good at fixing things. That's where you come in.

You'll definitely want some great posters and flyers. Check the quick section at the end of Part One – 'How to spread the word!' on page 57 – for how to do that really well.

Make a list of the things you can do: mend chains, fix punctures, remove rust and so on. It might be a good idea to ask your local bike shop if you can spend a day there for free to get work experience and learn more about maintaining bikes.

Think about whether you are going to do mobile repairs or if people will drop their bikes off at your house.

Please don't fix bikes if you don't know how to. You quite literally have someone's life in your hands. One cog thing (or whatever they're called) out of place and someone could have a horrible accident.

If you know your stuff, you'll soon get into a cycle of good customers.

(I'm very proud of my puns in this book.)

What you need to do this job:

★ Puncture repair kit (more tools if you choose to offer more maintenance)

★ Shed, garage or other covered space to work in if customers drop bikes to you

9. SELLING FRUIT SALADS

I love mangoes. If you love mangoes too, or any other fruit, then selling fruit salads could be the money-earner for you!

There are great profits in selling fresh food and fruit salads are very easy to make.

Head to your local supermarket or market and buy a variety of fruit. Generally avoid anything out of season as it will be expensive – but you do need a splash of colour to make your salad bounce off the shelves. A handful of strawberries, raspberries, blackcurrants or black grapes will add this colour.

Buy some clear plastic bowls, small tubs and forks too.

At home, start preparing your fruit salad. You will need to research how to make it truly mouth-watering and the best way to prepare the fruit.

Summer fetes are a great place to sell fruit salads. There are lots of rules about selling street food. You can't just set up a table at your local shopping centre, for instance. Think about where you want to set up your stall and then ask the relevant people if this is possible.

If you have your sights on more than the local school fete, you may need to get a food hygiene certificate. You can find information about this on your local council's website.

Maybe have two sizes – small and large – or offer a selection of toppings such as cream. Delicious!

What you need to do this job:

★ Fruit

★ Containers and plastic or wooden forks/spoons

★ Toppings

★ Signs

★ Tablecloth

WAYS TO EARN MONEY INDOORS

10. A CAKE SALE

A cake sale is one of the easiest and best ways to make money.

You can either rent a table at a sale that someone else has organised or you and some friends can organise your own. The first thing you'll need to do is find a venue. I recommend a community centre, village hall, sports hall or local school. Write to them or go and speak to them. Ask how much it would cost to rent out their space for a few hours. They'll come back with an estimate of how much it is going to cost to do what you've planned. Also ask if they have tables to put the cakes on.

At this point you'll need some leaflets and posters! Check the quick section at the end of Part One – 'How to spread the word!' on page 57 – for how to ace that.

Now think about how many cakes you may need. After you've come up with a rough estimate, bake or buy your cakes. I mention buying cakes because there is quite a good profit in doing it this way and it's perfect if you can't cook.

At a fundraising event I did last year, I bought a huge chocolate cake from my local supermarket for £8. I managed to cut it in to 12 slices and sold each slice for £1.50. That means the cake sold for a total of £18. After taking off the £8 I paid, that left a £10 profit.

But it's much more satisfying to bake your own cakes. There are so many yummy recipes, so you can be really creative.

Try making plain small cupcakes, setting up a table full of icing and sprinkles and charging people £1 to decorate their own cake. People are happy to pay more for an activity. Also, this means you don't need to spend so long preparing your cakes. Your customers are paying to do it for you.

What you need to do this job:

★ Ingredients for your cakes

★ Napkins or paper plates

★ Signs

★ Tablecloth

★ Sprinkles and other cake decorations

11. SELLING YOUR CLOTHES AND UNWANTED ITEMS ONLINE

eBay

eBay was my second ever attempt at earning some money. It's so simple but so effective.

The great thing about eBay is whatever you're selling, you sell it the same way. This means that you'll get the hang of it really quickly.

You need to be 18 to have an eBay account and therefore you will have to ask a parent/guardian to set one up and allow you to sell on theirs.

You can also sell items for other people and charge them a commission. For instance, they could give you a pair of jeans to sell for them on eBay and you agree to half the money that they sell for. (After all, once sold, you will have done the hard work of photographing, measuring, listing them and posting them out.)

To start, you'll need to find your items, then research the prices at which you should sell them. Have a look at similar items on eBay and what prices they are selling for. Have they got any bids on yet? If they haven't, maybe they are too expensive.

Let's say I bought a book for £10 – I might think about selling it for £5. Don't always halve it, though. The price depends on a few things. The first is the overall value of the product, the second is the condition, and the third is when you bought it. If the book is rare, in great condition and selling well – I could charge more. (But if it's common, tattered and unpopular, I might get less.)

Getting this right depends on the product. For instance, if you're selling a medal from the second world war then the price gets higher the older it gets. If you're selling a product that's a current craze, then as the craze dies out the value will go down.

Let's get into the actual selling of the product.

Start with going onto **ebay.com** or **ebay.co.uk** and creating an account. Once you've done that there should be a button that says 'Sell'. Click that and type in the name of your product. It will come up with suggestions. Click the one that suits your product best.

Afterwards press 'Continue' and type in the title that you want your product to be displayed under. You can only use 80 characters in the title – *I recommend that you use them all*. This is because you'll be able to include more keywords so that when a customer searches there's more chance of your listing coming up.

You'll see an option for a subtitle but you don't have to put one in if you don't want to. After you've decided on a title you'll see a dropdown box titled 'Condition'.

Make sure you're totally honest about the condition of your product. Then you can upload some pictures of the product.

Make sure the pictures that you take look great and are appealing. The picture is the first thing that people see, so that and the price will be – to a great extent – what they make their decision on.

Then there are more options that you can select if you want to, but they aren't compulsory. After that you need to add your description.

Make sure it's not too long but not too short. For the book I was talking about earlier, I might add the blurb on the back and maybe some of the reviews. Then you need to select whether you want to 'auction' your product or sell it for a 'fixed price (buy it now)'.

The auction means that people will try and win your product by bidding for it. You'll add a starting price and an end date. The bidders will (hopefully) keep putting the price up until the end date. This means that you may get more money than you asked for. Incidentally, on competitive items, experienced eBay users often hold their bids back until the last few minutes (or seconds) of an auction – so you can't always tell how it's done till it's over.

If you want a fixed price, all you need to do is enter it in. This means that you'll get exactly what you asked for if someone decides to buy your item.

Remember, eBay has to make money too. They'll take a percentage of the money that you make.

Once all of your details are in you'll need to add postage/shipping. As a customer I love free shipping, so you could build that into your price.

Don't be upset if someone doesn't buy your item, it just means that they're looking for something else or they've found a better price. I would try and compete with the other items out there to try and get the best deal.

Have fun!

Pepop – selling unwanted clothes

Depop is like a mixture of Instagram and eBay. It's a great way to sell unwanted clothes and an even better way to quickly earn some money!

You have to be 14 to have a Depop account, so ask a parent/ guardian if you can sell on theirs if you are younger.

To start, go on to **depop.com** or download the Depop app on your phone or tablet.

First, press the 'upload' button. Upload a photo, title, size and price – and that's all you need.

Add postage and a payment method and watch your Depop empire grow.

Maybe your Depop shop will look as good as the clothes you're selling!

12. BABYSITTING

Babysitting is another traditional way to earn some money.

This requires a lot of trust and responsibility.

I think to start with it would be a good idea to sit for children and families that you know. If you are familiar with the house and know the child, it will make life easier.

You can run your babysitting service any time: weekday evenings, weekends or even in the daytime during school holidays.

There are lots of online courses you can do for first aid and accident procedures. It would be sensible to do a course so that you know what to do if ever needed. This will also show the parents that you take your job seriously.

Once you have decided on your hourly rate, let families know about your sitting service.

Always take down their contact numbers before they leave and agree when they will be back.

Below is the official UK guideline regarding the age at which you can babysit:

> "There is no minimum age at which children in the UK can be left on their own, nor do laws specify how old someone needs to be to babysit. However, if the babysitter is under 16, then the parent remains legally responsible for the child's safety."

What you need to do this job:

★ Diary

★ First-aid basic training (advised)

13. HELPING OTHERS WITH ONLINE SHOPPING

It can be hard for less mobile people to go to the shops and buy everything they need, whether it be clothes, food or gifts.

My grandmother was one of these people. She always tried really hard to keep up with birthdays and Christmases but sometimes couldn't go out without struggling.

We thought of a solution for her. Online shopping. However, she grew up in a world where computers didn't exist and she had no idea how to use one. Now just before you jump to conclusions, no, I did not charge my own grandmother money to shop for her. But what I'm thinking is that if you know your way around an online shop and live in an area with older people, helping them with their online shopping could be a great way to earn some extra money.

The chances are that they are paying someone to go and get their shopping anyway. This way they can join in the shopping experience and maybe see new products and price changes.

I would charge per hour but have a minimum price per shop. If you have cycled 15 mins and the shop only takes 10 minutes, it might not be worth your while.

This is a quick way to earn a bit of money but it requires you to have a lot of patience – like my grandmother, you may get a full explanation each week of why they need their Maynards Wine Gums!

The last thing to say is that helping an older person with their shopping is something you may just want to do for free to help them out. If they're anything like my grandma, the people you help will make sure you get some kind of reward for helping, like a cup of tea or some wine gums.

What you need to do this job:

★ Laptop

14. TEACHING AN OLDER PERSON HOW TO USE A COMPUTER

This follows on nicely from my last idea. Older people have not grown up in a technical world and can find it all very daunting. We've already talked about online shopping but wouldn't it be great if they could connect with their friends via Skype or FaceTime or watch BBC iPlayer to catch up on a show they've missed?

So they might ask you to teach them how to use a computer, tablet or phone.

Again, there isn't much to say about the job itself, it's more the preparation and execution. To start with, sit down for a couple of hours and write a lesson plan, something to prompt you on what to teach them.

Maybe something like:

> 10:00 – How to find your way around your desktop

> 10:25 – Using the Internet

> 11:00 – Online shopping

> 12:00 – Social media

> 13:00 – Gaming (if they're that sort of person!)

They might also ask you to help them choose the right equipment for them and get you to set it up for them. Be flexible as everyone is different.

It's the posters / leaflets / flyers note again! Check the quick section at the end of Part One – 'How to spread the word!' on page 57 – for how to do that really well.

Perhaps visit a care home or retirement village and ask the staff if they can hand out your leaflets to residents.

Set an hourly teaching rate.

Remember, for this job you'll need to know your way around a computer and be very patient. This might be an older person's first time using a computer so they'll have to get used to it.

What you need to do this job:

★ Your own technology if they don't own anything yet

15. PETSITTING

If babies aren't your thing then I know just the job for you!

Petsitting is a fun way to earn some money.

Start by asking your parents/guardians if you can have a pet such as a dog, cat, mouse or bird staying in the house. Other pets, such as a rabbit or guinea pig, can live in the garden.

If they say yes, that's great!

Petsitters need posters! *(And flyers.) Check the quick section at the end of Part One – 'How to spread the word!' on page 57 – for how to get that sorted.*

For this I would set a daily rate, not hourly. People are going to want you to take care of their pets for maybe a week or so, so you don't want to have to work out how many hours the pet has been in the house.

Before the animal is left with you, make sure you get clear instructions on how to care for it. Ask the owners for the phone number of their vet, just in case the animal becomes ill.

What you need to do this job:

★ Garden if you are caring for outdoor animals

★ Permission for animals to live in your house

★ Clear instructions about the care of the animal

16. MAKING AND SELLING ART

Art. What a fun way to earn some money.

'Artist' is such a big word. It could mean being a painter, caricaturist, landscape artist, doing pottery or working with textiles. If you decide that this is what you're going to do, you probably have some art skills already, so I won't talk about the job itself.

Once you've made a couple of products (I would maybe make five or so) you need to find a way to sell them. The question is how. Well, the first would be to ask your local council if you can sell on your street but that's quite risky in terms of customers. There'll be a real difference in customer numbers depending on where you are. If like me you live in a very quiet, isolated, rural area then you probably won't get many customers at all. However, if you live in London, New York or any other big city or town you should have no problem meeting customers.

Remember, you can't just rock up on the pavement: you must ask a parent to get in touch with the council or government first.

A car-boot sale is also a great place to sell and showcase your work. Then there's eBay, summer fetes – or even your local garden centre, homeware or gift shops. Ask them if they can stock a few.

Often cafés and pubs will let you hang paintings on their wall with a price tag on the frame. They get their walls decorated and make some commission every time they sell one for you.

Until you share a gallery with Picasso, make sure that your work is at a sensible price. Research what similar pieces are selling for.

What you need to do this job:

★ Your own artwork

17. BE A YOUTUBER

Being a YouTuber is the hardest way to earn some money, but if it works you can earn a lot!

Why is it so hard? Because there are billions of videos on YouTube. Three hundred hours of video are uploaded to YouTube every minute and almost five billion videos are watched on YouTube every single day.

If you find a gap in the market, something that no one else is doing, then I can almost guarantee you that you're either doing something incredibly cool and entertaining or something bonkers.

On YouTube there are no right or wrong answers. Just mess around with stuff. Have fun! I mean, people can make millions by uploading a video of a cat falling off a fence!

If your channel gets over 10,000 views then YouTube gives you the option to start making money. You just have to activate the 'monetise' button.

Keep your content fresh and you may just be on the road to Viral City!

What you need to do this job:

★ A phone, tablet or computer to film and upload video content

★ When you're more established you may need editing software, lighting and a microphone

18. UPCYCLING

Upcycling is one of the most creative ways to earn some money. All you need is a box of old or unwanted clothes, furniture or even plant pots and whatever springs to mind to customise them.

Firstly, let me just explain a bit about what upcycling actually is.

Let's say you've got a pair of jeans that you don't need anymore. Sure, you could just sell them as they are, but maybe you want to do a bit more.

If you customised your jeans you could sell them for a much higher price. This could be by sewing badges onto them, tearing them up (if you're in a destructive kind of mood), sewing buttons and beads onto them or maybe even turning them into a comic strip with fabric pens.

Once you've decided on what you're going to do, you can begin! Remember to take your time to maximise the value.

One thing that I forgot to mention is that upcycling isn't just clothes. It can be furniture, book covers, plant pots or phone cases.

Once you've rejigged your items, they're ready to hit the shelves. You could use eBay to maybe get more than you originally wanted. Or there's Depop, the online clothes specialist. There's also another good site called Etsy. Then there are car-boot sales and local markets.

There are so many ways for you to upcycle and sell. Get creating!

What you need to do this job:

★ An item to upcycle

★ Materials and crafts to upcycle it

19. DESIGNING AND MAKING FIMO CHARMS

Fimo clay always has a place in my heart (no, my heart is not made of Fimo clay). It has a place in my heart because it's partly how I got inspired to start my business Not Before Tea.

My mother had a business called Sherbet Pip, which as well as selling sweets, sold necklaces of little pretend sweets made out of Fimo clay – it's a very soft and easy-to-use clay that bakes hard in the oven.

All that you need to do is go to a craft shop or any place that sells craft materials and buy a few packs of coloured Fimo clay. Go home and start making your models, jewellery, charms etc. Put them in the oven for however long the packet says, and take them out when they're ready. Let them sit and then they're ready to be sold!

You can make magnets, jewellery, badges, key rings and much more.

This is a really social thing to do too. Maybe invite your friends round and you can all create together.

When it comes to where to sell, eBay, Etsy and local fetes are all good places to start.

What you need to do this job:

* ★ Fimo

* ★ Craft accessories such as jewellery ends and badge pins

* ★ Oven

20. PHOTOGRAPHY

Photography is another creative way to earn some money. And the great part about it is that you only need a phone or camera.

Think about what interests you or what is around you. A friend of mine keeps chickens and takes the most amazing photos of them.

Try to specialise in one thing: flowers, people, animals, buildings, cars and so on.

Take the photos and either keep them as natural photos or play around with filters and get a bit more contemporary.

There is so much you can then do with the images:

1. Print them off and buy some mounts and sell them as prints. If you don't have a good printer, use a service online to print them.

2. Sell the rights to the image online. Upload your photo to the likes of Shutterstock and people will have to pay you a fee to use the image. You could get quite a lot of sales from just one photo.

3. Get going with merchandise: turn the photos into calendars, mouse mats, mugs or cards. There are lots of websites where you can do this, such as Snapfish, Vistaprint and Photobox.

What you need to do this job:

★ Phone or camera

★ Mounts and cello to sell the prints

★ Printer (if you want to print your own things – just check that it's not cheaper to use a website)

21. WRITE A BOOK

Whether you write biographies, short stories, novels or poetry, becoming an author could be a way to make a bit of money. Sure, someone like J. K. Rowling's success is one in a billion, but it's still a way to earn something. You just have to go in with your eyes open: around 200,000 books are published in the UK every year – that's more than 20 an hour – and the vast majority are only bought by a handful of people.

How do you start? An idea. What makes for a good idea? The key is to think about who your readers are going to be. If a chef cooks food in a restaurant, his menu has to be things that people will order. He can put his own twist on things (in fact, that's how he'll get known) – but he can't just cook what he wants: not if he expects people to turn up, pay and come back.

So think about who you want to buy your book first. Look at what they're already buying. And then make sure your book does what they want – with your own twist, of course.

Now you need to put your thoughts down in writing. Some writers like to discover their way to their structure. Others like to plan every detail. Others are somewhere in between. Find what works for you – the key is to try and avoid wasting time going in the wrong direction.

Then get going! Set yourself a weekly word target, share drafts with readers you trust for feedback, polish until you're sick of the sight of Microsoft Word – and you've put the odds massively in your favour.

Once your book is written you have a few choices:

1. You can get a publisher for your book. This can be really hard (even J. K. Rowling struggled at the beginning). The good part about getting a publisher is that they will do everything for you in terms of editing, designing and producing the book (they will expect you to work with them to promote it). The bad part is that you can lose control and only get a small percentage. You need to find one that you trust and get along with.

2. Self-publish the book. This is what I did with *The Adventures of Sherb and Pip*. I did it all through Google: found a local printer, found a designer, got my barcode for the back and registered with the British Library. There is a huge section on marketing your business later in this book (see Part Three), and that will give you lots of help for promoting it.

3. Find someone online such as Lightning Source that does print on demand (the book only gets printed when someone buys it). Amazon has its own print-on-demand service called CreateSpace but be warned: if you give your book an Amazon CreateSpace ISBN, some independent booksellers will refuse to sell it – even if a customer requests it.

4. Don't forget about eBooks! If you look online there are some helpful guides to formatting and uploading your book for sale on eBook platforms. You might also want to explore audiobooks!

What you need to do this job:

★ A computer

22. VIDEO EDITING

Someone has some footage that they want editing but they don't know how to edit. Perhaps it is of their wedding, party or holiday. You can edit it, set it to music and turn it into a great memory for them to treasure. All you need is a computer or tablet and a video editing app.

iMovie is an easy editing tool but can produce really professional videos. Pricing for this is difficult. You may want to charge per minute of finished product or per hour editing. It's up to you. (But agree it before you edit!)

You'll probably be liaising with your customer via email but if the file they are sending is too big for email, try other tools like WeTransfer or simply post a memory stick.

What you need to do this job:

★ Computer

★ Video editing software

23. CUSTOMISING T—SHIRTS AND MERCH

Customising T-shirts and other merchandise is a classic way to make some money.

There are great websites out there like Spreadshirt and Camaloon which do a wonderful job printing T-shirts, clothes and other accessories.

All you need are some art skills or a catchy slogan/quotes and you can get them printed.

Think about what you're going to do and what you're going to do it on.

You might start with, say, ten T-shirts, five mugs and five hoodies. Go online and find a great place to get them made.

On Spreadshirt there's a feature where you can publish your work on their site and people can then buy through them. You don't need to dispatch the order or buy huge quantities. They'll make them as people order. I would definitely recommend that.

You can also try the old-fashioned methods of tie-dying or screen printing blank garments at home – messy but great fun! Or even design using fabric pens.

If you want to sell direct, try having a stand at your local market or setting up a website and selling your designs from there.

What you need to do this job:

★ Computer to do your designs

★ Garments to get your designs printed on

24. PARTY ENTERTAINER

Entertaining at parties covers so many different skills under one umbrella. Whether it is face painting, puppet shows or even putting your babysitting skills into action (see '12. Babysitting' on page 36), there are many ways to earn some money in this field.

To start, find out when a friend or family member's wedding, birthday, Christmas party or other get-together is taking place. Ask if they need any help looking after the children or helping entertain them. If they say yes, you've just got a customer!

As with most of our jobs so far, work out an hourly rate and make sure your customer is OK with it. Give them a list of services that you can offer that will help entertain the children.

If you are serious about being a party entertainer, it is a good idea to do short courses on balloon modelling, basic magic and party make-up. You don't have to be able to do all of these things, but the more skills you have, the more likely it is that people will be interested.

When it comes to the event itself there is something you must remember: you are being paid and need to do what the customer has asked for, not join in the party.

If you are serious about this job, you might want to enhance your skills and learn how to face paint, juggle and other cool party tricks.

Hopefully at the end you may get a slice of cake!

What you need to do this job:

★ Equipment depending on the type of entertaining you are doing

25. GIFT WRAPPING

If you've ever wanted to be an elf, this is the job for you.

To be an elite gift-wrapper, you require pointy ears and bells on your shoes. Just kidding – but it might help!

To start, make sure you know how to wrap really well.

It's not just wrapping paper you'll need – get some posters and flyers too! Check out the quick section at the end of Part One – 'How to spread the word!' on page 57 – for how to do that really well.

When it comes to pricing, you might want to charge per gift, not necessarily per hour.

Offer to visit someone's house for a morning and do all their wrapping for a set price. You can offer to bring the paper and ribbon with you or use theirs (charge accordingly – paper and tape can be expensive).

When you do get a customer, make sure you really try your best with the wrapping. I understand from my friend, who wraps at a big department store in London, that the art is to use as little sticky tape as possible and to practise your bows!

What you need to do this job:

★ Tape

★ Scissors

★ Wrapping paper

★ Gift tags

★ Ribbon

26. TEACH A MUSICAL INSTRUMENT

If you play a musical instrument, sing or conduct then teaching someone those skills could be the job for you. Now I know, if you are young, there will be teachers with far more years of experience than you – but that doesn't mean you can't make a difference by helping someone learn. Some children actually respond better being taught by someone closer to their age.

The first thing you must think about is *where* you are going to teach. Do you have facilities in your home that you can use? This may be a piano, or a spare room that you and your pupil can rehearse in. Make sure that you have basic equipment like two music stands, suitable seating for the instrument you're teaching, and the correct accessories like spare guitar strings or rosin for violins, mutes, endpin stoppers and the like. Alternatively you can be mobile and visit customers in their homes and teach them on their instruments.

If you are teaching someone to sing, make sure you have a piano or keyboard for warm-ups and accompaniments. Make sure you know your music theory as well!

The important thing with teaching is to be patient. Not everyone will grasp things as quickly as you, so keep calm and try your hardest to teach around them. Ask them if they prefer going over and over things, or to try things slightly differently. Build your lessons around your customer.

Do your pupils want to take their grades? To teach ABRSM music you most probably

need to be on a very high grade yourself. Always teach lower than your grade.

What you need to do this job:

★ Instruments if your pupils don't have any

27. DESIGN AND SELL PIN BADGES

Designing and selling pin badges is another really creative way to earn some money. And it's great fun as well.

To start you need to create your design or identify the object to go on the front of the badge. This could be Fimo clay, wood, knitted items, gemstones, shells, felt pictures or even bottle caps.

Then you'll need to get some safety pins or pin-badge backs and really strong glue to attach the badge back to your decorative item. You can get all these from a craft shop or eBay.

You can sell them pretty much anywhere – a car-boot sale, online or at craft fairs.

What you need to do this job:

★ Decorative items

★ Badge backs

★ Strong glue

28. MAKE SOFT TOYS

Making soft toys – a knitted bear, a sock toy, a ragdoll – is an excellent way to earn some money.

Find something like a sock, a shirt, a bobble hat or anything that's soft, and sew or glue buttons or other bits and bobs onto it. You may want to buy some stuffing online to fill it with. Once you've filled it, sew or glue it up and it's ready to sell.

You could also make puppets or other toys out of obscure items.

You can sell them online, at markets, fetes or even in your local gift shop.

It is very important to think about the age of the child that the soft toy is designed for. Small items like buttons and beads are choking hazards for babies and toddlers and some stuffing can be dangerous too. If you are worried, put a label on saying 'Not suitable for young children'.

What you need to do this job:

★ Materials to make the toys

29. RESCUING BOOKS

For this method of earning some money you'll need a helicopter and a siren (maybe a rope ladder as well).

Well, OK, maybe we're not going to be doing *that* kind of rescuing. But the results can be almost as exciting.

To start, go to a charity shop or market and find some old books. Look for books that are not in great condition – maybe they have lost their covers or someone has scribbled on a few pages. These books will be very cheap to buy (maybe even free).

We're going to be upcycling – but for books. There are many things you can do – not only with the illustrations (if they have them) but also the words.

You could cut pages into strips and glue them over items such as boxes, pots and lampshades. You could cut around the illustrations and stick them onto blank greetings cards. Something that has been very popular over the last few years is taking a really great page and putting it in a frame. People can no longer enjoy a damaged book so this is a great way to give the illustration a second lease of life – and for you to make a bit of money.

To sell them, you can go to a market, a car-boot sale, online or to your local gift shop.

What you need to do this job:

★ Old damaged books

★ Frames/blank cards

★ Scissors

30. DRAW CARTOONS

Drawing is a creative way to earn some money – and the possibilities are endless.

You can draw electronically or in your sketch pad and then turn them into electronic form (by scanning).

You'll want to make a really loveable character or a not-so-loveable villain for your audience to get behind. After you've designed your characters, put their adventures on anything from standalone illustrations to full comic strips.

You can then make copies and turn the illustrations into prints, cards, T-shirts, mouse mats, posters or electronic products such as screensavers.

You can sell your products at markets, online, in gift shops (or even one day at Comic Con!).

What you need to do this job:

★ Sketchbook

★ Way to convert your illustrations to electronic files

★ Blank items to turn your designs into merchandise

HOW TO SPREAD THE WORD!

Later in the book I've got some expert advice on marketing your business (see 'Marketing basics' on page 121). But for these quick ways of earning some money, you don't need that level of activity.

What you will need, though, are some quick, cheap ways of spreading the word.

Because this comes into so many of the ways you can make money, and I want you to be able to jump around the book as much as you like, I thought it made sense to cover how to do that in one place – here!

Design

When it comes to design, go for simple and eye-catching. Take time. Be creative.

People don't want to read forever so stick to the basics. If you're offering your services say **what** you can do, how much it will **cost**, and how to **contact** you.

If you're setting up a car-washing business, you can stick to describing your services as (drum roll) 'CAR WASHING'.

If bike repair, you should say 'BIKE REPAIR', but you should also list the sorts of things you can fix. Just use common sense – if you were a customer, what would you need to know before committing?

If you're running an event, say **what** it is, **where** it is, **when** it is, how much it will **cost** and how to **contact** you.

There have been countless occasions where I look in shop windows and some poor person has written a 300-word essay. No one wants to stand and read a long leaflet. Say what you need to say. Nothing more.

Distribution

Good places for posters and flyers include:

★ village or town halls

★ community centres

★ newsagents' windows

★ supermarkets (they often have noticeboards by the tills)

★ bus stops

★ sandwich and coffee bars

★ local shops (if you're not competing directly!)

You'll have to get permission – it's obviously not a great idea to stick up posters somewhere they're not allowed when they have your contact details all over them! But people are usually happy to let you stick something up or leave a pile of flyers – and if they're not, just move on and try elsewhere and don't take it personally.

On a flyer, you might want to add a bit about you and why you're offering your services so that you stand out from junk mail and other flyers. But not too much. Brief is best!

Don't bother putting leaflets under car windscreen wipers. It just annoys people. And they throw them away.

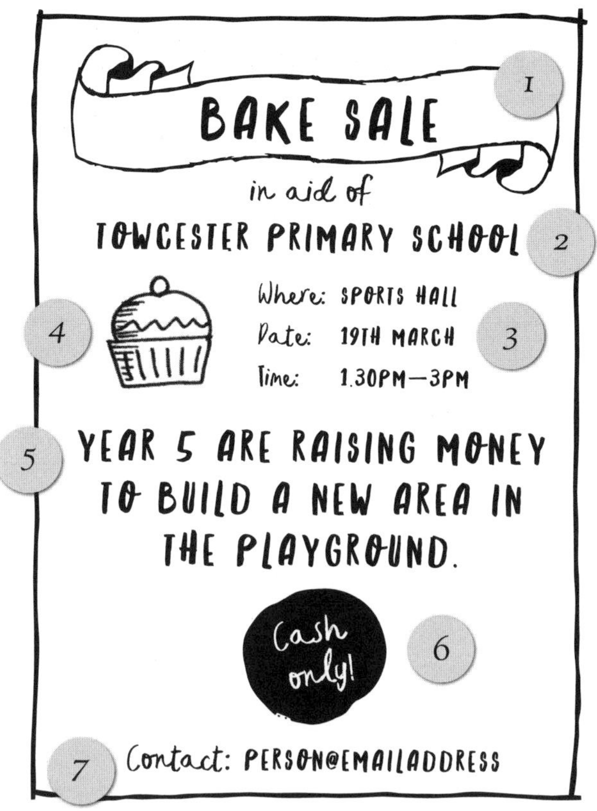

1. Title that is big and bold to draw the attention of readers.

2. Who you are raising money for. Could be a charity, place or person.

3. Details about where and when the event is taking place.

4. Images relating to fundraising.

5. Who you are and why you are trying to raise money.

6. Any details that would affect anyone attending, such as types of payment accepted or where the best place to park is.

7. Contact details for anyone who wants to find out more information.

SELLING YOUR STUFF — EVERYTHING YOU NEED TO KNOW

Something else that comes into many of the ideas in this part of the book is *where* to sell stuff. I suggest suitable places with each of the ideas, but wanted to gather some more detailed advice and links too!

Online marketplaces

Online marketplaces are websites that will sell your items for you – once you've written the description, uploaded photos and set the price. When it is sold, you post the item to the customer. These places either take a cut or charge to list items – check a site's terms when setting up!

There are lots of marketplaces all around the world. Here are just a few to get you started. Web addresses change over time, and you may be based anywhere around the world, so it's best to do a web search to get straight to the right page for the marketplaces where you live. Note that you need to apply to join some of the examples listed below.

★ Amazon Marketplace

★ ASOS

★ Depop

★ eBay

★ Etsy

★ Folksy

★ Hard to Find (Australia)

★ Noon

★ Not on the High Street (UK)

★ SHWRM

★ Zibbet

Markets and car-boot sales

There are markets, car-boot sales and pop-up events happening every day – you just need to keep an eye out in your local paper or 'what's on' guide. During Christmas and summer, most villages and towns will have fetes and shopping evenings – normally the price of having a stall at a local event is very low.

County fairs and exhibitions

There are many permanent exhibition centres that hold shopping events on a large scale. Often they are sponsored by a TV show or magazine and they get thousands of visitors through the doors. A stand at these events can be expensive, but it's worth it if you can sell enough.

Shops

The most common way to sell products is through shops. You sell your product to a shop at a certain price called the 'wholesale price' and then they sell it to their customer for a bit more (the 'retail price').

Pricing is a very big area but I will give you a rough guide to working it out. Let's say you make jewellery:

1. A bracelet costs you £2 to make (beads, chain, clasp and little gift box). Note – *you never have to tell anyone this figure.*

2. You sell the bracelet to your local gift shop for £4 – this is the wholesale price (you have made £2 profit and doubled your money).

3. The gift shop will then sell the bracelet for, say, £8 – this is called the retail price. They have made a £4 profit and doubled their money. Note that they can charge whatever they want for your bracelet.

The gift shop has not only found you a customer but also has plenty of fixed costs to pay like rent and electricity. Even though you made it, it is fair that they also make money when selling your bracelet.

If you approach a shop and show them your products they will ask you what your wholesale price is. You now know how to work it out. They will also ask you if it comes in any packaging, such as gift boxes and how quickly you can make more if they want to make another order.

You might be expected to supply your products on 'sale or return'. This is where the shop has the right to return unsold items to you for a full refund.

Your own website

You can build a website with an online shop very easily and cheaply these days. My first online store for Not Before Tea was built through Shopify. I just chose a template and it was really easy to upload my products and change the colour scheme to make it feel like my store. It is free to get started and then you just pay a small amount each month – it is like you are renting your online shop. They also take a small amount of money every time you sell something. However, it really is a great way to get trading quickly.

You can also use WordPress to build an online shop. This isn't quite as simple as the likes of Shopify but if you know someone who is good with techie stuff, this will be cheaper in the long run as you don't have to pay commission or monthly costs.

Photographing your products

Whether it is for eBay, your own website or for your leaflet, if you sell actual products, you will need to photograph them.

A good photo will sell the product and a bad photo won't. The good news is that cameras on phones are so good now, the chances are that you can get some decent pictures of your products to get you started.

Before you start, look at some big brands who sell similar products to you. How do they position and photograph their products?

Here are three top tips when taking your pictures.

1. **Lighting** – Without the right equipment it is hard to take good product shots indoors. If you have a very well-lit room, that is great. If not, head outside and place your product on a painted piece of wood or piece of fabric. You can buy A3 background sheets that look like marble, planks, brickwork and much more – they are very good. No one will know they were taken outside and the light will be much better. Don't choose a very sunny day, though, as you will get too many shadows in the picture.

2. **Background** – Keep the background clean and simple if it is an item of clothing or something that requires clean lines. However, if you are photographing a tweed bag, you might want to hang it on a country gate and have some of the background in shot.

3. **Props** – Don't be afraid to use props. If you are selling greetings cards, maybe put a smart pen next to it. If you sell jewellery, a huge grey pebble with the jewellery hanging over it can look very effective.

Having a stall/stand

It doesn't matter if you have a pitch at the local car-boot sale or a stand at a huge international event, your display must be brilliant. I would always sell from a table, not a mat on the floor, as it is easier for people to pick up and look at your products.

Here are my other tips for selling at an event:

1. Your pricing must be really clear. Use smart string price tags or chalk boards, not horrible ripped pieces of paper.

2. You don't have to have a tablecloth if your products are contemporary but often the tables you are given at these events are quite ugly. Think of how you will cover yours.

3. Think tall! You can buy some very cheap folding shelves that can sit on your table to give you more display space and make your products really stand out.

4. Bring a chair – it is exhausting standing all day.

5. Lots of people will pay with notes so bring lots of change. I also try to keep all my prices at a rounded pound or 50p. That way I just need to bring £1 coins and 50ps for change.

6. Bring a notepad to scribble out a receipt if customers ask for one. The receipt should briefly describe the item sold, the price paid and the date.

7. Have plenty of business cards and leaflets as some people might not want to buy now but follow up later.

8. Can you accept card payments? You will find people buy more if you can take cards. I have a little machine from iZettle for Not Before Tea and it works via Bluetooth with my phone. The money then goes straight into the business bank account.

9. Bring a supply of pens, Blu Tac, a calculator and snacks to keep you going.

An example of a good advert or leaflet advertising your business or service:

PERSONALISED POTS
BY AMY

My personalised ceramic pots make great
thank you gifts for teachers and for that special present
at Christmas and birthdays.

Simply choose your pot size, colour and message to be
hand painted on the front and I will get creating!

(A GOOD PHOTO GOES HERE)

PRICES START FROM £12 FOR A SMALL POT

PLEASE ALLOW 7 DAYS FOR YOUR ORDER TO BE MADE

POSTAGE: £4 PER POT

TO ORDER PLEASE EMAIL: AMY@EMAILADDRESS

OR VISIT MY WEBSITE: WEBSITEADDRESS

If you want to order in person, I have a stand at the
Woburn Craft Market on the first Saturday of every
month, so pop along and see the whole range.

PART TWO:
20 Ways to Fundraise for a Good Cause

There are so many people who are worse off than you and very often just raising a small amount of money can do great things to help them.

Whether you want to earn money for your school or club, or help communities worldwide, in this part of the book I have gathered together some of my favourite and easiest ways to raise funds.

You can get ideas on how to advertise the events in the marketing section at the end of Part One (see 'How to spread the word!' on page 57). But for fundraising, you also mustn't forget to get your local paper involved – they love to report on events for good causes.

1. ART ATTACK

You will need:

★ A table

★ Some judges

★ A score sheet

★ A computer and printer for posters

How it works:

1. Start by thinking of a theme for your art competition, such as Disney, food, animals or travel.

2. Create some posters to let people know you are running an art competition. You need to make sure you include important information such as the deadline for submissions, where to bring submissions and how much it costs to enter.

3. On the day of judging, grab your table and set it up so people can place their submissions on it. Make sure they have paid to enter the competition. It is also important to make sure people's names are on their artwork (and age if you have sections). Allow the morning for people to arrive and display their art. Then at lunch clear the room and invite the judges in to view.

4. Ask the judges to use their score sheets to rate each submission.

5. Once the judges have scored all of the submissions, look at which one got the best results and announce the winner. A prize could be an art set or voucher at the local art shop.

Additional way to raise money

At the end of the day you could auction off each painting, with all money going towards your charity (make sure the artists are happy with you doing this first).

2. BAG PACKING

You will need:

★ Collection buckets

★ Lots of volunteers

How it works:

1. Contact a local shop and ask if you can go in on an allocated day to make money for charity by offering to pack people's bags. The best way may be to visit the store itself.

2. Once you have been approved, grab a bunch of friends, some money collection buckets and head to the shop.

3. Then simply ask people at the cashier if they want you to pack bags for them. If they say yes then off you go. Make sure your team know which items go together in each bag.

4. Make sure your bucket is clearly displayed so people know to donate money if you have packed their shopping bags.

Remember...

People are kindly paying for you to do a job they could probably do themselves. Take extra care with items such as eggs and bread – no one wants them squished!

It may also be important to plan ahead. Times of the year such as Christmas could be more lucrative due to the amount of shopping people do. But you should also take advantage of unexpected events – a heatwave, for instance, seems to make people in the UK go mad, buying far too much food for BBQs and parties, which could result in more customers.

3. CHARITY QUIZ

Everyone loves a quiz, making it a great way to raise money for a favourite cause. People can pay to enter and, depending on numbers, either play as individuals or in teams. Choose general knowledge questions so that everyone who plays will know some of the answers. Don't make it too specialised or it may not suit everyone. I wouldn't be much use in a sports quiz, for instance.

You will need:

★ Lots of questions

★ Prizes

★ Paper and pencils

★ Chairs and tables

★ A microphone (or very loud voice)

How it works:

1. Find a good place to host the quiz. This may be a school sports hall, village hall or a pub. Anywhere with enough room to host a large group of people.

2. Now you need to write the questions. There are hundreds of free quizzes online which you can use or you can make one of your own. Make sure you have a mixture of easy and hard questions on a range of topics.

3. In order to make money, you need to sell tickets. This can be done individually or to groups.

4. On the night, you will need to set up tables with enough chairs to fit a team around. Spread pieces of paper and pens about to allow people to write down their answers.

5. If you are hosting the event in a large space, make sure you have someone with a very loud voice or a mic reading out the questions so that everyone can hear them.

6. Once you have all the results in, announce the winner. It may be nice to give one prize to the winner and one to the runner-up.

7. At the end, make sure you dispose of the rubbish and put everything away. If you leave the venue in a mess you may not be allowed to do a charity quiz next time.

Additional ways to raise money:

As well as having people participate in the quiz, you could also:

★ Serve tea/coffee/drinks as people are doing the quiz and charge them a small amount.

★ Run a small raffle that could be done while answers to the quiz are being checked.

Remember...

It may be a good idea to have one person going around the tables checking that people aren't looking up the answers on their phones. Nobody likes a cheater!

4. CHARITY CAKE SALE

Cakes and baking are very popular at the moment. Most people can bake a cake and everyone loves eating them, so you should have no trouble getting help to produce the sale items or in persuading people to come. Make sure you let them know that it's for a good cause too.

You will need:

★ Table

★ Napkins

★ Paper plates

★ Plastic cutlery

★ Plastic cups (if you are serving drinks as well)

★ Lots and lots of cake

★ Price labels

★ Money pot with some change

How it works:

1. Firstly, find a suitable location for the cake sale – somewhere visible, where people will easily be able to find you.

2. Create posters to advertise the event. Remember the tips from the section at the end of Part One ('How to spread the word!' on page 57)! The key thing (other than enticing people to come and buy lots of cake for a good cause) is to remind people to bring money in for the cakes, and to ask people to donate cakes to sell.

3. Set up a table at your location and spread the cakes out, making sure the prices are clearly displayed. Give someone responsible the duty of handling the cash.

4. All you need to do now is sell. Make sure you have people going around letting anyone and everyone know that you are selling cakes.

5. At the end of the sale, make sure you dispose of the rubbish and put everything away. If you leave it in a mess you may not be allowed to do a cake sale again.

Remember...

You will need to label any cakes that may contain nuts. This is important – if someone with a nut allergy eats nuts in one of your cakes it could cause them to become ill. Sometimes it is best to avoid selling any cakes with nuts in them, but you should warn people just in case.

5. CHRISTMAS GIFT WRAPPING

Some people love wrapping Christmas presents but others find it a chore, especially if they have a lot of relatives to buy for.

You will need:

★ Tables – see if you can borrow fold-up tables from your local village hall or school

★ Scissors – several pairs

★ Tape dispensers

★ Coloured pens

★ Portable music player – a bit of Christmas music helps set the mood

★ Wrapping paper – different patterns for different age ranges

★ Tissue paper

★ Ribbon

★ Rosettes

★ Raffia and fancy string

★ Gift tags

How it works:

1. There are lots of places you can set up a gift-wrapping station. On the high street, ask permission in shopping centres or department stores (prior to the day). You could also enquire with your local town hall or community centre (if they're not too far from the shops). Alternatively, if you are prepared to wrap up warm, you can always set up in the street itself – with British weather it's guaranteed to be a bit cold, but you would attract attention.

2. In a busy location, people may not see or read posters! But printing flyers and getting a friend or family member to hand them out near popular shops will advertise your services directly to customers on the day.

3. Set a clear pricing list. This could be based on either the size or shape of the presents. Alternatively, you could just be open to a donation per gift. It may also be a good idea to give incentives to customers with a deal – e.g. five gifts wrapped for the price of four.

4. Be merry! Christmas shopping is stressful at the best of times. Be considerate of people's time. You could even wear elf ears or a Santa hat to add to the festive spirit!

Remember...

If you are someone who can't wrap presents, put the sticky tape down – this fundraising idea might not be for you. If you are all fingers and thumbs, team up with a friend/family member who can wrap while you focus on attracting customers and taking the money.

6. CRACK THE SAFE

'Crack the safe' is a good challenge because it's quick for each person to take their turn and it's likely to take hundreds of turns before anyone guesses the code. In fact, it's likely that no one will win the prize – but it doesn't matter as it's all in a good cause. You can let people know that if no one wins, the prize will be donated to your charity as well.

You will need:

★ A prize for inside the safe

★ A small plastic safe with a three or four-digit combination code

How it works:

1. Place the prize in the safe and lock it.

2. Ask people to pay to have one go at cracking the code on the safe. If they don't crack it, they can pay again to have another try or let the next person have their turn.

3. If they do crack the code, they win the prize inside. Make sure you place another prize in the safe and change the code so more people can have a go.

4. If you don't have a small safe, place the prize in a plastic tub. Get someone to think of a three-digit code which can be used to open the plastic tub. Get people to write on a piece of paper what they think the three-digit code is – and if someone gets it right, open the tub and give them prize. Then repeat step three.

Remember...

Change the code once someone has cracked it.

7. EATING COMPETITION

An eating competition is another fun, food-related way to raise money. Just make sure that it's suitable for the cause concerned. It wouldn't look right to hold an eating contest to raise money for starving children, for example.

A novel twist might be to use healthy food, such as carrots and broccoli. Though ensure that people still want to enter! Or you could add a rule that you are only allowed to use chopsticks or are not allowed to use your hands. This would make the event more fun by creating a bigger buzz and attracting more contestants.

You will need:

★ Food (of your choice)

★ Tables and chairs for the contestants

★ A pot to collect the money

★ Napkins

★ Water

★ Rules

★ A prize for the winner

★ A stopwatch

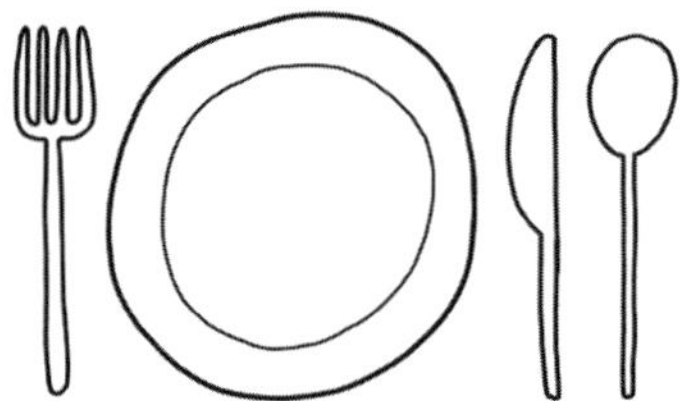

How it works:

1. Find a local store, bakery or restaurant willing to donate some food for the occasion.

2. Set up your tables and chairs so the contestants have a place to eat.

3. Lay out the food for each person and establish the rules.

4. Collect the money from the contestants.

5. Whoever can eat the most in the time limit wins the prize.

Additional way to raise money

As not everyone will be taking part in the competition but may still be hungry, you could also have a stall selling food and drink. This probably isn't the time to try the broccoli idea, though.

Remember...

Not everybody is able to eat the same food – it is against some people's religion to eat certain foods, or they may be allergic. You need to take this into consideration when planning the event so that everybody can take part.

8. FACE PAINTING

Face painting is very popular at fetes and fairs as well as children's parties. It requires more skill than some of the other ideas. It will help if you have a talent for painting or drawing but anyone can give it a go. There are lots of instruction videos online where you can learn the techniques and get ideas for designs. You can also get books showing different designs that you can use on the day to let people choose their design while they're waiting.

Do remember to practise before doing it for real! If you don't fancy the painting part, find a friend or an adult who has done it before. Ideally you should have a team of two so that no one has to wait too long for their turn and so the face painters can take a break from time to time.

You will need:

★ Face paint (multiple colours)

- ★ Brushes

- ★ Sponges

- ★ Bowl of water (to rinse brushes and sponges)

- ★ A supervisor

- ★ Stencils/book of designs

- ★ A mirror

- ★ A towel

- ★ Hair bands/clips

- ★ Glitter

- ★ Chair

- ★ Table

How it works:

1. Lay out your equipment – brushes, paint and glitter. Make sure your brushes and sponges are clean. Fill up a bowl of water in order to clean your brushes and sponges.

2. Hand your customers the design book so that they can choose what they want while they are waiting for their turn.

3. Once they have decided what they want you can begin to paint, using the colours and technique that you feel would be best.

4. After you have painted you should then show them how it looks to see if they are happy with it. If they aren't, redo it or go over the part they don't like.

Remember...

You need to take good care of your equipment so that you can reuse it. You also need to make sure that you only use proper face paint made to be kind to skin. If anyone complains of skin irritation you should remove the paint immediately.

9. HOW MANY SWEETS IN A JAR

You will need:

★ Some sweets

★ A jar

★ A clipboard, pen and paper to write down people's names and answers

★ A pot to collect the money

★ A prize

How it works:

1. Get an empty jar.

2. Fill the jar with some sweets (remember to count exactly how many are in there so that you know the total).

3. Ask people to take a guess at how many sweets are in the jar.

4. At the end of the competition, reveal the winner! If no one guesses exactly right, the winner is the one with the closest guess.

Additional way to raise money:

You can auction off the jar full of sweets at the end (if you haven't made it your prize).

10. LUCKY BIRTHDAYS

Anybody with a birthday can take part in this game. It is basically a raffle with a twist that makes it more interesting.

You will need:

★ Paper

★ Pen

★ Bucket

★ Prizes

How it works:

1. Draw up or print off a calendar of all 12 months of the year, showing every date.

2. Collect some prizes. The best way to do this is to ask family or friends to donate some.

3. Get some pens, some paper and the calendar that you created earlier. Get people to pay to have their birthday as their ticket. Slowly, the calendar will fill up.

4. Once you have got as many people to get a ticket as you can, write down all the birthdays that have been bought and put them into a small bucket or container.

5. Just like a raffle, take one ticket out at a time and assign it to a prize. Whoever bought that ticket wins the prize.

Remember...

Don't sell the same date twice. If someone's birthday has already been bought, suggest they buy the birthday of a family member, family pet, famous person or a historic day.

11. PET SHOW

Lots of people have pets and a pet show can be great fun for pet owners, anyone who likes animals and the pets themselves. My pug Martha always loves going to events where she can meet other dogs. Make sure you pick a suitable venue. There should be a supply of fresh water for the animals. Avoid anywhere too noisy which might frighten the more timid animals.

You will need:

★ A venue such as a village hall, a field, communal green or a school sports hall

★ A panel of judges; try to get people that the participants and audience will know – for example, a local mayor or a head teacher

★ A prize for the winner and runner-up

How it works:

You can run the pet show in various sections:

1. Small animals (rabbits/hamsters/tortoises)

2. Dogs

3. Unusual animals (such as lizards)

4. Most talented pet – open to all

5. Pet that looks most like its owner

6. The judges will judge the section and present the prize at the end of each one.

Additional way to raise money:

You could also sell refreshments.

12. RECYCLE RUN

A recycle run is a good way to raise money by encouraging people to take exercise while having fun dressing up. I must admit it probably wouldn't be my first choice as a fundraising idea because I'm quite a slow runner, but we can't all be Sir Mo Farah. All ages and abilities can take part and do it at their own pace.

You will need:

★ A large space, such as a field or a park to host the run

★ Some rope to mark out the start and finish line

★ Medals to award the winner and runner-up

★ A whistle

★ Some volunteers to help direct the participants

How it works:

1. Find a good spot to host the run. A large field or a park would be best. You want the participants to be running no more than 5 km. You could get people to run to the top of a hill and then back down, along a section of a nearby beach, around a school playing field or through a town centre.

2. The point of a recycle run is to get people to dress up for the run, but without spending any money on their costumes. This will get people creating costumes out of recycled clothes and packaging.

3. The next step is to get people to participate. Get them to sign up by paying their entrance fee and giving them a number to stick on the front of their costume.

4. Mark out the start and finish line and place volunteers around the course. This is so they can point the volunteers in the right direction. You will also need someone to see who is the first person to cross the finish line.

5. Grab a whistle, count down from five and off people go.

6. Once everyone has crossed the finish line, award the winner and the runner-up their medals.

Additional ways to raise money:

As well as charging people to enter the race, you could:

★ get people to be sponsored to participate in the event

★ get people to pay to have their costume judged and award a prize to the best one

★ have the volunteers going around with buckets asking anyone around to donate money.

Remember...

At the end, make sure you dispose of any rubbish and put everything away. If you leave the area in a mess you may not be allowed to do this activity again.

13. RUBBER DUCK RACE

A rubber duck race is my kind of sport because most of the hard work is being done by someone else – rubber ducks in this case!

You will need:

★ Lots of rubber ducks

★ Waterproof pen

★ Whistle

★ A river/stream with a marked-out start and finish line

★ A net to catch the ducks at the end

★ Some volunteers

★ Blackboard/clipboard to take entries/sponsors

★ Pens/chalk

★ Long stick to poke any ducks that go astray

★ A prize for the winner

How it works:

1. First, collect all your rubber ducks and number them on the bottom with a waterproof pen. This will allow you to keep a record of who has sponsored which duck. You will also need to create a list or spreadsheet to collect the names and contact details of people who have sponsored ducks.

2. Mark out the start and finish line of the race and place a large net at each end. This will allow you to hold the ducks back at the start, ready for when the race begins, as well as allowing you to collect them at the end.

3. Once everyone who wants to has sponsored a duck, place the ducks at the start line and make sure everyone knows the race is about to begin.

4. With two people holding the first net at the start line, start a countdown – then blow your whistle. This signals for the net to be lifted out of the water, and for the race to begin. If you start on a bridge, you can simply tip the ducks over the edge in a bucket.

5. As the ducks flow down the river, it may be that people walk down with them and you may want a volunteer to push ducks back into the race with a long stick if they get caught in weeds or stuck at the edge.

6. Like any race, the first duck to cross the finish line wins. Make sure you have someone ready to pick it up quickly, as many ducks could cross the finish line close together and you don't want to get confused about which duck was first.

Additional ways to raise money:

As well as having people pay to sponsor the ducks, you could also:

★ hold a competition to guess how many ducks took part

★ serve drinks/food (running after ducks can be hard work)

★ hold a design-a-duck competition – for a fee (and with a small prize on offer) let people decorate their ducks before the race.

Remember...

Being by a river or stream can be dangerous. Make sure there are plenty of people around to keep people safe and make them aware of the river edges. Only ducks should be in the water!

14. SPONSORED GIVING—UP

All of us have something we could give up because it's bad for us or because we could live without it. A sponsored giving-up is a nice way to encourage people to help themselves and others at the same time.

You will need:

★ Sponsorship form

★ You could use a funding website

How it works:

1. To raise money for charity, you could get people to sponsor you to give something up.

2. Examples of things you could give up include: complaining, saying no, food such as sweets, talking, and spending money on things you don't need such as clothes, the Internet or electronic devices.

3. The way you raise money is to decide what to give up and how long to give it up for. Create a sponsorship form and get people to pledge to give you money if you manage to do it.

4. One of the ways that you can get people to sponsor you is to use sponsorship websites. An example is **justgiving.com**.

Remember...

You are giving something up for a good cause, so no matter how tempted you are to stop, try your best to keep going.

15. SPONSORED DOING

People can be sponsored to do anything. It helps if you choose something you like and that you're good at. Set yourself a challenge – people are more likely to sponsor you if they can see that you are doing something hard.

You will need:

★ Sponsorship form

★ You could use a funding website

How it works:

1. To raise money for charity, you could get people to sponsor you to do a specific activity.

2. Examples of activities that you could get people to sponsor you to do could be extreme sports such as sky diving, running in a marathon, completing 24 hours of a specific activity such as dancing, or eating a certain amount of food such as 25 bananas in 15 minutes.

3. Decide what you are going to do and when you are going to do it. Create a sponsorship form and get people to pledge to give you money if you manage to do it.

4. One of the ways that you can get people to sponsor you is to use sponsorship websites.

16. SCAVENGER HUNT

Everyone loves an Easter egg hunt. This is a version of the same idea that you can do at any time of the year.

You will need:

★ Something to hide, such as sweets or chocolates that are in wrappers. If you do this at Easter you could use mini chocolate eggs.

★ Bags to give your hunters something to put their goodies in.

How it works:

1. Find places to hide your sweets/chocolate. Good places could be a classroom, garden, school field or playground. Put some posters up telling people where to go for the hunt and how much it will cost them to join in.

2. Hide all of your sweets/chocolate, making sure no one who is doing the hunt can see where you are hiding them.

3. Give all the hunters a small bag in which they can put the items they find. This makes it easier for them to hold things and hunt for more.

4. Once all of the hunters have finished and can't find any more treasure, bring them back and tell them they can eat the treasure they found. You could give a prize to the person who found the most.

5. Make sure you do a check over the area where the hunt took place to pick up any rubbish and check that all the sweets/chocolate have been found.

17. PENALTY SHOOTOUT

Sporting contests are always popular and a penalty shootout is easy to organise, doesn't need too much space and is exciting to take part in and watch.

You will need:

★ A football goal

★ A football (and a spare in case it gets lost or punctured)

★ Goalkeeping gloves

★ Scoreboard/sheet

★ Whistle

★ Money box

★ A float (coins and notes that can be given as change)

★ Winner's prize

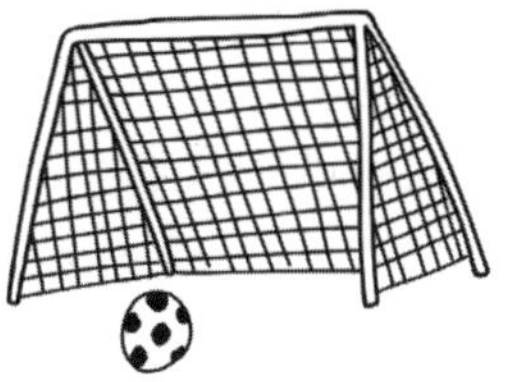

How it works:

1. Decide where to hold your penalty shootout. It could be a local park, school field or sports centre. You may need to book it.

2. Promote your event. You can do this by making posters and putting them up around school or on your local noticeboard. If you're over 13 years old and have a Facebook account, you could even create an event on there. This way you can invite specific people in your area or make it open to the public.

3. Choose a great goalie! The idea of a penalty shootout is to get participants hooked and determined to score. If they score easily they won't need to pay for as many turns, which defeats the purpose of your fundraising idea.

4. Each contestant has five turns at a time. Make sure to take note of people's scores (and their name and contact details).

5. At the end of the event, see which person scored the most out of five and give them their prize! In the event of a tie, have a penalty shoot-out with each person taking three more turns until there's a winner.

18. TALENT SHOW

We recently organised a talent show to raise money for our drama society to put on a musical production. We used the money we raised to buy the scripts and hire a venue. The great thing about a talent show is that you can guarantee that everyone who takes part will have friends and family who will want to come and cheer them on, so it's easy to sell tickets.

You will need:

★ A venue such as a village hall, a school sports hall or a pub (somewhere with electricity).

★ A sound system of some kind and adequate lighting.

★ Someone who understands technology to run the sound and lights, if any.

★ A panel of judges. Try to get people that the participants and audience will know. For example, a local mayor or a head teacher.

★ A prize for the winner and runner-up.

How it works:

1. Once you have chosen your venue, decide if you are going to split the talent show according to age. Perhaps you can have 12 years and under, 13 to 18, and 18 plus.

2. Hand out as many leaflets and posters as you can and invite people to enter via post or email. It is better to get people to enter in advance so that you can prepare the programme.

3. You will need a presenter, someone who will host the evening and introduce each act.

4. The panel of judges can sit at a long table, in front of the stage, just like on *The X Factor*. If there is no stage, sit them to one side or they will block the audience from seeing the show. Ask the judges to score each act and then add up the scores at the end. You don't need to share all the scores with the audience – just announce the runner-up and winner.

Additional ways to raise money:

★ This works very well as an evening event, so you can sell refreshments at the interval and also have a raffle.

★ Perhaps start the show with a fancy-dress competition for the little ones (charge per entry).

Remember...

Make sure anyone performing lets you know what they're doing – if they need a backing track/music then you can sort that out for them if possible. There is quite a lot of organising involved, so maybe put someone in charge of requirements for each act.

19. TOY AND GAME SALE

Most of the toys and games we buy end up in cupboards or taking up space in our bedrooms. Organising a sale is a great way to recycle the things we've outgrown. You will find mums and dads like this idea too, because they get a tidier house.

You will need:

★ A collection of old toys or games

★ A pot to collect the money

★ A stand/table where you can display the toys or games

How it works:

1. Have a sort through of your games and toys and decide which ones you want to sell. Ask your friends to do the same.

2. Print leaflets and posters to advertise where and when your sale is taking place.

3. Out of the ones that you have selected, give each one a price. You might want to consider how popular each one will be or what condition they are in.

4. Display your toys and games on the stand so that people can see what you are selling.

5. Get selling!

Additional ways to raise money:

★ Sell refreshments

★ Hire out tables so other people can sell their toys and games too

Remember...

Some games have age restrictions, so you'll need to use your best judgement when selling your items so that you don't sell to anyone who is underage.

20. WET SPONGE THROWING

This is just great fun!

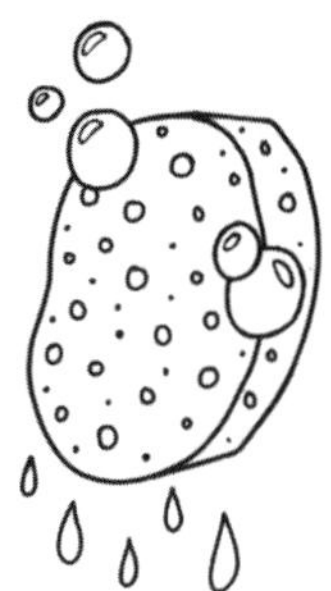

You will need:

★ A bucket

★ Wet sponges

★ A hose or tap to refill the bucket

★ Willing volunteers

★ Towels

★ Some kind of headrest for the victim to support their chin while they're getting bombarded

How it works:

1. Find some people who will be willing to have wet sponges thrown at them. If you are doing this at a school, it may be worth getting your head teacher as most people would be more than happy to throw sponges at them.

2. Get a bucket and some sponges. Fill the bucket with water and make sure the sponges are soaked.

3. Find a good location to hold this activity. It will probably need to be done outside as there's a lot of water involved.

4. Now the activity can begin. Make sure people don't stand too close or they will be able to hit their target easily. People have to pay for every sponge they throw.

5. If the volunteers get cold, make sure you give them a towel and allow them to dry themselves. (Just be sure you have someone else ready to have the sponges thrown at them.)

6. At the end, make sure you dispose of the rubbish and put everything away. If you leave the venue in a mess you may not be allowed to do this activity again.

Remember...

Make sure the sponges are clean. It would be horrible to have dirty sponges thrown at you and may discourage people from participating.

PART THREE:
How to Turn an Idea into a Business

The question I get asked more than anything is what advice I would give to someone wanting to get started in setting up their own venture.

As you'll hear me say more than once in this book, having a stand at a car-boot sale is my number-one tip for learning the basics of business (see '3. A pitch at a car-boot sale' on page 21).

Once you have got some initial experience, you are ready to start developing your real business idea. To get us started, I have asked my business mentor (and good friend) **Jodie Hughes** to talk us through the basics.

BUSINESS BASICS

By Jodie Hughes,
Entrepreneur acceleration manager,
NatWest

HOW CAN I TELL IF MY IDEA IS A GOOD IDEA?

So many of the entrepreneurs I have worked with have assumed that other people will love their idea because they came up with it and they think it's the best thing in the world. They then go and spend lots of money producing it and when they try to sell it no one wants to buy it because they haven't actually found out if there is a problem to solve.

Every idea comes from what we call a **pain point**.

A pain point is the reason the customer chooses you/your product. The point when they realise that you/your product gives a solution to their need or 'pain'.

For example, reusable water bottles were created so that people could carry water with them to stay hydrated, re-fill them and save money (and the environment) by not buying water from shops. The pain points they solved were that people need water when out and about and hate buying bottled water because it's expensive and bad for the environment.

Activity: *Take five minutes to work out what problem you are trying to solve. For example, you like to play football at the weekends but you often find that your teammates get really hungry after a match. You decide to start a tuck shop where you sell tasty snacks to your teammates after a game. You are solving their hunger problem!*

A guy called Steve Blanks came up with the **Customer Discovery Model,** which is when (with a basic idea in mind) you go out and find out what your customers want, then you tweak your idea to meet your customers' needs (or you pivot if they don't want what you are offering).

Pivoting is simply a change in direction to your original plan. For example, if your idea is a bright green chocolate bar and you go out and speak to your potential customers to ask for feedback and most of them say they would hate to eat a green chocolate bar but would love a purple chocolate bar, changing to create a purple chocolate bar could be seen as a pivot.

To do this you need to be brave, get out of your bedroom and ask your potential customers what they want.

Make sure you ask a variety of questions – some will be closed questions with a yes or no answer, and others will be open where you ask for their opinion and they can say whatever they like. The main point is to get out and ask people what pain points they have before spending too much of your well-earned pocket money on a product you haven't tested.

> **Your second activity:** Think of ways to find out what your customers want. Could you put together a questionnaire for your potential customers to fill out?

TURNING MY IDEA INTO A BUSINESS

OK. You have done your customer discovery and have found that people want your product. That is an excellent start!

The next step is to get planning. I could suggest writing a business plan but they take a long time and as start-ups change quickly your business plan is soon outdated, so here are a few questions to consider before starting your business:

Think about your customers:

★ What's their pain point?

★ Who are they?

★ Where do they hang out? (This can include online.)

★ What value are you offering them? (Essentially, what's important to them – quality, price, convenience?)

★ How much are they willing to pay?

Manufacturing:

★ How are you going to get your product made?

★ Are you going to make it from scratch?

★ Are you going to outsource it? (This means getting someone else to make it for you.)

★ How many products do you need to make/buy?

Marketing:

Having a great product is a good start but if no one can find it then what's the point?

★ How are you going to get people to know what your business does?

★ What forms of advertising are you going to use? E.g. leaflets, social media adverts.

★ Have you set aside any budget for marketing activities? Leaflets cost money to design and produce.

Finance:

★ What budget do you have? (How much money do you have to start your business?)

★ How much does it cost to produce/buy your product?

★ How much do you want to sell your product for?

★ What other costs do you need to consider?

Sales:

★ How are you going to sell your products? (In shops, online, at events?)

★ Will you be selling them or will someone be doing it for you? (You will have the most passion for your business and this is really important when trying to sell at the start.)

Distribution:

★ How are you going to get your products to your customers once they have bought them?

★ Will you hand deliver, send via post or outsource it? (Remember to include this in your cost of goods sold.)

Customer service:

★ What happens if something goes wrong with the product? Who deals with it? How do they contact you?

★ What if a customer doesn't like their product and wants their money back? Who deals with it?

LEARNING ABOUT FINANCE

Don't be scared of the maths involved when starting a business. I thought I was really bad at maths at school which made me hate it. Not liking numbers really impacted negatively on my first business because I decided to ignore them rather than see them as an exciting element of being an entrepreneur.

The numbers within your business tell the truth – they tell you whether you are making money or whether you are losing money.

You need to know how much it costs to make your product to then work out how much you should sell it for.

When you know this, you can then decide whether it's worth putting the hard work in or whether it's best to look at a different idea.

JODIE'S JARGON BUSTER

Revenue or sales – when you sell a product the money that you get is called 'revenue' (or sales). For example, when you go to a shop and buy a bottle of juice for £1, the shop receives £1 from you. This is called revenue. If you bought ten bottles of juice, the shop would get £10 of revenue.

Cost of goods sold (COGS) – this is how much it costs to make your product. For example, if you want to make a bar of chocolate, the costs to make the physical product will include the ingredients (like milk, cocoa, sugar), the packaging and everything else. Don't forget to include staff costs.

For example, maybe you are paying your friend to help you on your cake stand at a local fete for three hours. You are paying her £10 in total and you have 200 cakes to sell. £10 divided by 200 cakes is 0.05p. You must add this 0.05p to the cost of the flour, icing sugar, chocolate and also the price to be at the fete.

Activity: *Take a moment to list down the costs involved in making your product. You can easily search some of the costs online if you are unsure.*

Gross profit – this is the money you make after deducting the cost of goods sold (COGS). It's a really simple sum:

Revenue – COGS = gross profit

For example, if it costs 50p to make a bottle of juice and the shop sells it for £1, then the gross profit would be 50p.

Fixed costs – these are all the other costs associated with the business that are not dependent on the product. For example, if you sold no bottles of fizzy juice there are still some costs that you would need to cover, e.g. rent, staff and marketing. At the early stages of your business you probably won't have any fixed costs but it's very important you know about them.

Net profit – this number shows whether you are actually making any money. The net profit is the number left after all your costs are taken away from your revenue. It's a really simple sum:

Gross profit – total fixed costs = net profit

For example, we know that the COGS of a bottle of juice is 50p. We also know that the shop sells it for £1. Let's say the fixed costs are 5p. Therefore, our net profit is 45p.

50p – 5p = 45p net profit

Loss – when you make a loss it means that you aren't making any money. It means that your total costs (COGS and fixed costs) are higher than what you are selling the product for.

For example, if we changed the fixed costs in our original example to 60p, what would happen to our net profit?

Gross profit – total fixed costs = net profit

50p – 60p = –10p

We have made a loss because it costs us more to make the product than we are selling it for. This is why it is so important to understand the numbers behind your business. You can then make the right pricing decisions for your product so you don't make a loss.

Let's look at this exercise on a table:

	Per product
Revenue (how much money you sell your product for)	£1
COGS (how much it costs you to make the product)	50p
Gross profit (how much money you have left after you have removed the cost of making the product)	50p
Fixed costs	
Rent of your studio	5p
Net profit	45p

Example: *You want to sell a book for £5. It costs you £2 to make the book. You also have £4 of rent to pay as you are selling from a corner of your local bookshop. What's your net profit? (Answer is -£1). Do you think that is a good business model? No, it isn't. You have actually lost money. But what could you do to make it profitable?*

Well, there are a few things you could try. Ask the owner of the bookshop to reduce the rent you have to pay. If you only had to pay £2 rent then you would make £1 profit. Alternatively you could sell online and you wouldn't have to pay rent at all. However, sites like eBay will charge a fee to sell your book, so you will have to include this.

This is a very basic way of understanding whether it's worth pursuing your business idea. Remember, there are ways to reduce your costs (e.g. cheaper ingredients) but you can also increase your prices. If a selling price of £1 doesn't make you enough money then consider increasing your price – you must make sure your customers are willing to pay a higher price, though, which can be asked when you are finding out who your customers are and what they are willing to pay.

WHAT DOES BUDGETING MEAN?

Often when people start a business they get really excited and start spending the initial money they have in the business – you need to make sure that you **budget** at the beginning. Budgeting is when you work out how much money you have and how much you want to use in the business.

For example, if you have saved £50 of pocket money and birthday present money you could use this. Next you must work out what the absolute essentials are that you need to spend the money on. Can you buy a small amount of product to start with, sell it and then put the profits back into the business?

This is a really great way to start but you need to be really strict with yourself and make sure you don't just spend the profits – if you want to build a business you will need to learn to sacrifice.

It's also important that you don't spend money on creating a product that people don't want – this is where you customer research comes in handy again.

You could produce a **minimal viable product** (MVP), which is a basic version of your product so that people can get an idea of what you want to achieve. Henry is great at this – he created a MVP out of his Mum's old coat and used other bits and bobs from around the house when he presented the idea to me. He could then show me an actual product instead of me trying to imagine it.

Starting a business and bringing your ideas to life is great fun. I am so excited to see yours in the future!

BRANDING BASICS

By Clare Yarwood-White,
Branding Director, Opal & Co

My favourite game to play at Christmas is the Logo Board Game. How amazing is it that you can see a corner of a logo and know instantly what brand or company it belongs to?

Here is **Clare Yarwood-White**, *who has helped me so much with the style of Not Before Tea, to tell you all you need to know about turning your idea into an award-winning brand...*

WHAT IS A BRAND?

What do you think of when you hear the word **brand**? Does it make you think about world-famous brands with iconic logos like McDonald's, Nike or Apple? Or does it make you think of people, such as Joe Sugg, Kim Kardashian or David Beckham who actually live and breathe their own brand?

A brand can belong to a company or an individual person. Either way, branding is basically all about the **messages** you send out about your business. Your audience uses these messages to build up a picture about you and decide if they want to buy from you. You need these messages to be clear, consistent, and really exciting for your customers.

WHY DO I NEED A BRAND?

Why do you need a brand? Quite simply, to make it easier for people to buy from you. A strong brand will help you:

1. Stand out from your competition

With over 50,000 new businesses starting up in the UK every month, customers have plenty of choice. An exciting brand will show them what makes you really special and help you outshine your competition in a crowded marketplace.

2. Attract customers who really love what you do

Lots of people will never buy from you. Don't panic! These people are not your target audience so you don't need to worry about them. Luckily plenty of people will love what you do and want to buy over and over again. A clear brand will help these people discover you more easily.

3. Make your marketing easier and more effective

You will need to make many marketing decisions as you run your business: decisions about the design of your website, what to post on social media, where to advertise, and many, many more.

It never stops! A consistent brand will stop you making the wrong decisions and will save you time, money and mistakes on your marketing.

WHAT ARE MY BRAND MESSAGES?

There are many types of brand message. Some are really obvious – for example, your company name, your logo, your choice of colours, and what you write on your website. These all clearly say something about you. However, there are other messages which are a bit more subtle, and can sometimes slip out without you really thinking about them. These not-so-obvious brand messages can include the way you treat your customers, the choice of products you supply, or how environmentally friendly your packaging is.

Below I've listed some of the messages a customer might use to judge your business before they decide whether they want to buy from you, or if they will buy from you again. There will be more. Circle those that you think are most important to you, and see if you can add in any that are specific to your business. By being aware of all the different ways you are communicating, you can control these messages better. This is sometimes called being **on-brand.**

★ Your logo

★ How often you update your Instagram

★ ....

★ How long you take to reply by email

★ The style of your photography

★ ....

★ Your choice of colours

★ How helpful your website is

★ ....

★ What your packaging looks like

★ ....

★ The font you use

★ Where you advertise

★ Who else uses your product

HOW DO I START CREATING MY BRAND?

So you start with the business name and the logo, right?

NO!!!

Sorry to shout, but this bit is really important because it's the most common mistake people make with their brand. There are some other things you need to think about before you decide on a name and a logo. In fact, the name and logo are actually just symbols of what your brand *really stands for*, so you need to work that out first.

You need to find a way to tell people what you stand for, or your **brand story**.

YOUR BRAND STORY

You might have heard people talking about their **elevator pitch**. This is something people in business use to help them tell their brand story. Here's how it works.

Imagine you get into a lift with your all-time biggest business hero, and you have 30 seconds to explain to them why your business is so great. You need to be clear about what you do and know why this matters to your customers. And you have to be able to explain yourself in just a few sentences; you have to get to the point quickly.

Sounds a bit daunting? Don't worry, I'm going to show you how to write your own brand story, and once you have done it, you'll find that elevator pitch an absolute breeze.

To write your brand story, start by answering the four questions below. Henry actually started his first business by selling bags of manure. To help you, Henry has answered the questions below, using this business as an example.

1. Why are you starting this business?

Think about what or who inspires you, why this business matters to you, and the unique talents or experience you have. This is your **brand vision** – it helps explain why you are bothering to run this business, and should convey your passion and energy.

Henry here! Where we lived we always had an endless supply of hot, stinky horse poo. When I discovered people would PAY for this (they put it on their flowerbeds to help the plants grow), I realised I wasn't sitting on a muck heap, but a gold mine. I could turn poo into profit! It was great to use my entrepreneurial skills on something that was so easily available to me. I couldn't resist.

2. What is your business going to do?

What business are you in, and how are you changing or improving the way similar products or services are supplied? This is your brand mission – it tells us what the core purpose of your business is.

I was selling manure in bags, which wasn't a new idea. But I was the only person on our road doing it, so it was very convenient for local gardeners. I also worked extra hard to make sure that only manure went into the sacks. No rubbish from the yard – purely poo.

3. How would you describe your business?

Circle the words below that best describe your business, or add some more of your own.

Ambitious	Calm	Detailed
Approachable	Clear	Distinctive
Artistic	Clever	Dramatic
Aspirational	Comforting	Driven
Authentic	Communicative	Earthy
Bold	Creative	Educational
Brave	Cutting edge	Efficient
Brilliant	Decisive	Elegant
Bubbly	Dependable	Elite

Energetic
Environmental
Expert
Fair
Friendly
Fun
Gentle
Graceful
Grounded
Hearty
High achiever
High end
Honest
Imaginative
Impulsive
Independent
Informal
Inspirational
Integrity
Intense
Intuitive
Lively
Logical
Luxurious
Methodical
Natural
Nostalgic

Nurturing
Optimistic
Opulent
Organic
Organised
Passionate
Perceptive
Perfectionist
Positive
Practical
Precise
Predictable
Productive
Professional
Provoking
Purposeful
Quality
Quick thinking
Quiet
Realistic
Reliable
Respected
Responsible
Results orientated
Romantic
Self-assured
Sensitive

Serious
Simple
Sociable
Soothing
Sparkling
Specialist
Spontaneous
Stable
Stand out
Strong
Substantial
Supportive
Surprising
Timeless
Traditional
Uncompromising
Understated
Unexpected
Unfussy
Unusual
Uplifting
Visionary
Warm
Welcoming
Youthful

Of all the words you have circled, group together those that have similar meanings (e.g. friendly, welcoming, sociable), then choose the three groups that are most important to you. These are your **brand values,** and set the tone for the personality of your brand. This is *how* you run your business.

My business was: **Friendly** *because I helped people put the bags in their car.* **Convenient** *because I made sure there were bags available seven days a week.* **High quality** *because I took time to make sure no rubbish went into the bags.*

BEWARE THE U-WORD

Avoid using the word *unique* to describe your business. You may well be one-of-a-kind, but unfortunately the word doesn't tell us anything at all about you. **It's one of the most over-used words in bad branding.** Instead of saying you are unique, try and find a word that explains *in what way you are unique* – this will be way more powerful.

So, now you know the *why, what* and *how* of your business, it's time to write your brand story. To do this you bring these three things together and make a promise to your customers about your brand.

PURE MANURE: *Pure Manure provides a convenient way to get the highest-quality manure for your garden. Only manure from our grass-fed horses goes into your bag, no sweepings or rubbish. Available seven days a week with friendly staff to help you.*

Now it's your turn.

EVOLVING YOUR BRAND IDENTITY

So now you have your brand story, you can start working on the elements that make up your brand identity.

1. Business name

Does your business name reflect your brand? If you have a fun brand, you can choose a witty name such as a pun or a play on words. If trust is really important to your brand, you might want to tone it down to something more sensible-sounding and reassuring. You don't always have to say what you do in your company name because if you have a strong brand this will come across in other ways. Short and sweet can sometimes be better.

Don't forget to check that no one else is using the name and if the web domain is available *before* you decide on a name.

2. Logo

Great logos are often very simple, but you can be very expressive with your choice of typeface. Don't be tempted to stuff too much into your logo – it doesn't need to have pictures or icons that show what you do. Aim to create something distinctive that reflects your brand style and will still look good when it is reproduced in different sizes and on different backgrounds. It's also useful to have a colour version and a black-and-white version.

3. Strapline

A strapline is a few words about your business that can appear with or without the logo, and sums up what you do.

4. Colour palette

Think hard about colour combinations that suit your brand personality. Lively orange and turquoise or calming green and grey? Sophisticated navy and gold or uplifting pink and silver? Choose around eight colours that you can use for backgrounds, headers, and other graphic elements. A range of dark and light tones will be most useful.

5. Fonts

Apart from your logo font, choose one expressive font for headers and key text, and another more simple font for main body text. Using the same font across all your marketing helps make it instantly recognisable.

Modern   Traditional   *Creative*

6. Writing style

Is your tone of voice chatty or authoritative? Informal is very fashionable at the moment, but it should suit the personality of your business. Make sure you are consistent. Don't use a chatty tone on your home page, and switch to stuffy legal-speak for your delivery information.

Two different ways to say the same thing:

★ Please ensure you order before 12 noon for next day delivery

★ Make sure you order before midday if you want it tomorrow

7. Photography and image style

Composition of pictures, lighting, props, subjects all tell a story about your brand. Find a consistent style that suits your products and your brand.

BRINGING YOUR BRAND TO LIFE

Now you have written your brand story and designed your brand identity, you are ready to start living and breathing your brand. It's your job to bring your brand to life in everything you do. Think again about your brand messages, and make sure all your communications (obvious and not-so-obvious) are on-brand.

Your ideal customers will now be hearing you loud and clear, and should start to recognise your business more easily. They will understand what makes you special and know exactly why they want to buy from you. They will even start telling their friends why you are so great. Congratulations, you have built a successful brand!

MARKETING BASICS

By Rebecca Patterson

Creating a good marketing plan for your business is essential. I have never paid for any advertising for Not Before Tea but I have done a huge amount of press and events to promote the products and get people talking about them.

Advertising is so expensive but luckily there are many ways you can spread the word about your business for free.

For the next section I have not had to look very far to get an expert to help, as my mother has had her own press and marketing agency for over 20 years.

Mother, over to you...

WHAT IS MARKETING?

Marketing is a process to introduce your products to potential customers. Without marketing, no one will know about your products or business and you will not get any customers. Lots of people think marketing is just one thing but this is wrong.

Think of marketing as a pizza with many toppings. Each topping is a different way of marketing: Instagram, for example, would be one topping, Facebook would be another. Others could be a stall at your school fair or a vlog.

Too many toppings on a pizza would be too much – it would be hard to eat (and rather messy). It's the same with marketing – you don't want to do too many activities to promote your business as you will probably end up not doing any of them very well.

There are so many 'toppings' that you can choose from; some you have to pay for and some are free.

Here are 35 ideas to get people to see your products or visit your website:

1. Newsletter – write a newsletter which will be of interest to your customers.

2. Put a poster up in shop windows.

3. Blogs – write your own.

4. Bloggers – get them to write about you.

5. Videos – make videos of you or your product in action.

6. YouTube – create a channel to host your videos.

7. Twitter – join relevant conversations and post interesting things about your business.

8. Facebook – you can build a community of interest around your brand. Anyone who follows or likes you online is a potential customer.

9. Instagram – people increasingly search for products online using images. Instagram is a great way to show people your products and establish a visual identity, the look of your brand.

10. Exhibiting – have a stall at an event where your customers will go.

11. Speaking – speak at an event about how your business and products can help people.

12. Emails – design some great-looking emails so you can contact your customers with offers and news.

13. Working with partners – do you know any people who can help promote your products for you? For example, if you sell hairbrushes you could partner with a hairdresser who can sell your brushes at their salon.

14. Text – this is a great way to give customers offers and news. Everyone looks at their phone!

15. Apps – create an app.

16. Balloons – give away balloons with your logo on.

17. Leaflets – traditional but still effective.

18. Sponsorship – sponsor an event, school event or charity. You don't have to give them money – you could give them samples of your products instead.

19. Appearing on TV – tell your story.

20. Appearing in magazines/newspapers.

21. Featuring on the radio.

22. Put your details on car stickers or T-shirts and walk around a lot!

23. Enter awards – then the awards organisation will promote you.

24. Word of mouth – get your friends and family to tell their friends about your business.

25. Get some really unique business cards made – and hand them out to anyone who might be a good contact.

26. Flashmob – know some creative friends? Organise a flashmob in your local shopping centre to attract attention.

27. Give away samples – this is great if you have a food business. Hand out a taster of your products. People will fall in love with the taste and will want to buy more!

28. Hold your own exclusive event and invite all your customers and potential customers to meet you and learn more about what you do.

29. Hold competitions where people can win one of your products.

30. Have a pop-up shop – some shops will let you have a small corner for the week to sell your products. If you don't ask – you don't get!

And if you are feeling crazy:

31. Get an airplane to write your logo in the sky.

32. Buy an airship with your logo on.

33. Organise a light show, spelling your business's name.

34. Climb Everest and photograph your logo on the flag.

35. Rent a billboard in Times Square.

When Henry first launched Not Before Tea we had no money at all for marketing so we had to put together a really creative marketing pizza... I mean plan.

We looked at the list of 'toppings' and chatted about which ones would work best.

1. We wanted to target mothers of children aged 2–5 and grandparents. This was our target market.

Action for you: *Write down who your customers are – this is your target market.*

2. We then crossed out all the 'toppings' that would not be suitable for our target market – for instance, most grandparents probably don't spend much time on YouTube.

Action for you: *Cross out all the toppings which would not be suitable for your target market.*

3. Finally, we discussed what we would do best. Henry loves filming and meeting people, so videos, speaking and events would be good. Don't choose something that you will find hard to do, as it is unlikely to work.

Action for you: *Write down what you are good at and what you enjoy.*

4. We then built his pizza. It is a good idea to choose 5–7 toppings. You need this many as sometimes they won't all work. For instance, if you are only relying on an event to meet customers and there is bad weather and the event is cancelled, you have a problem.

THE NOT BEFORE TEA MARKETING PIZZA

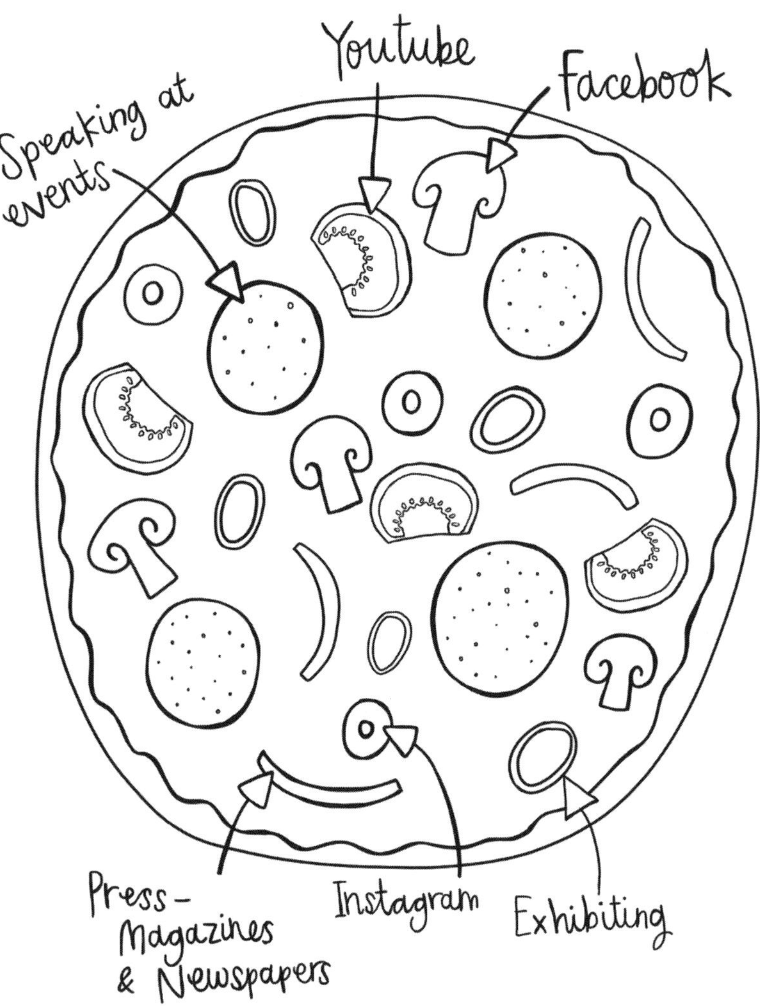

> **Action for you:** *Create your own pizza and toppings. (I really recommend that you choose featuring in magazines/newspapers as one of your toppings. I will explain why in the next section.)*

5. Once we had chosen our toppings, Henry needed to learn as much as he could about them. He went on an Instagram course, spent a day with a retailer learning how to display products, watched videos on how to make a great YouTube channel and watched lots of great speakers such as Steve Jobs to learn from the best.

Action for you: *Which toppings on your list do you need to learn more about?*

Congratulations – you have identified your top marketing tools for your business. The next step is using them.

GETTING FEATURED IN THE PRESS — WORKING WITH THE MEDIA

I am not going to go into detail about every topping on the list, or I will take up the rest of Henry's book, but I am going to explain how you can get featured in the press because I think it is such an important part of your marketing activity. It helps you create a name for yourself as an entrepreneur, your company and your products. The more people hear your name and read about you, the more confident they will be to buy from you.

When Henry was featured in the *Daily Mail* with Not Before Tea, 62,000 people visited his website in just one morning. It is very hard to find free ways to reach that many people in one hit and get them all to visit your website and buy your products.

Henry has appeared in over 200 magazines and news pages, which means that when you Google him or even the term 'young entrepreneur', there are pages of articles about him. Because of this, when a journalist Googles 'UK young entrepreneur' for a story they want to write, they will see Henry, interview him and another article is added to the list.

There are two big reasons why the press love writing about Henry:

★ He is young and has an interesting story.

★ He knows how they work and he knows how to talk to them.

There are two big reasons why the press will love to write about you:

★ You are young and have a great story.

★ You are about to find out how they work and how to do an interview.

The first thing you must do is make a list of all the magazines and newspapers who will be interested in either you, as a young entrepreneur or your business and products. Don't forget to include your local paper as they will be very keen to write a story about you.

The best way to do this is to go to WH Smith's (other newsagents are available) and look at all the magazines on the shelves. Which ones would your customers buy? There is no point in featuring in *Fishing Weekly* if you sell cakes and your customers love baking. Write down five to ten really relevant titles. Most people will read a newspaper, so look at those too. If you are aiming at young people, *First News* is a good paper.

Then go home and search for good blogs and online articles and add them to the list. Finally, add any radio stations and TV shows or news programmes that you think could be interested in you.

You now have your target press list. That was easy wasn't it?

Now you have to find out how to contact them. Try to get actual copies of all the magazines and papers on your list. The local library has magazines and I am sure your friends and family might get some too. Next go through each magazine and have a look at the type of articles they write. Where can you see yourself fitting in? If you design T-shirts you would be very relevant for the shopping pages. Often the publications have a 'meet the maker' page where they interview designers and entrepreneurs.

At the top of these articles there is a name of the person who wrote it. Have a look at the front of the magazine and often you will see, in very small writing, a list of the emails of the writers. If you still can't find the email address, ask your good friend Google.

Put all the contact names and email addresses next to the publication name.

You now have created your own press database.

Next you need to build your press library, so you have the right information to send the journalist.

Here is what you need to put together:

1. Photographs

I am sure you always look at the photos before reading the words, don't you? Having some good photos is really important. You need a photograph of yourself, including a head and shoulders photo and also one of you doing something related to your business. For instance, if you build websites, get a photo of you sitting at your computer. You don't need to pay a professional to do these photos. Get a friend or parent to take a photo on their phone.

It is important that the lighting is good and the image is interesting. Avoid taking pictures against a window or with the sun behind you, as you will appear very dark. Taking the shot against a wall covered in graffiti can be great. Don't get any photos against white backgrounds and avoid filters, cropping and flash. Most magazines want interesting colourful photos and will crop the images to fit the space.

Also, get some good photos of your products. Henry takes lots of his product shots outside as he doesn't have any professional lights. He has painted a wooden board white to put his products on for photos. Often the photos need a bit of work to make them look better, so he uses **www.fiverr.com** where you can get a photo editing service for just £3.50. You will need someone over 18 to open an account and process this for you. It is actually amazing what help you can find on there – and not just for photos. It's worth having a look.

If the newspaper sends their own photographer to take your picture, don't do anything you are uncomfortable with. I don't think a young person should ever look too serious. Smile and look like the creative and inspiring person you are.

I remember when Henry had his first shoot for a national paper. They came to the house and made him wear a bowler hat and stand with his arms crossed. The pictures were published and he looked frightening. They then sold the photos to other publications and this terrible photo

will haunt Henry forever. I should never have let them take the photos.

2. A description of you

Write a paragraph explaining who you are, why you started your business, why your business interests you, your plans for the future. Write about yourself as if someone else were telling the story (avoid using 'I'), like this:

> Young British entrepreneur Henry Patterson, founder of children's brand Not Before Tea (**www.notbeforetea.co.uk**), started his business journey at the age of nine, when he launched a collection of sweets including edible mud and worms. Henry went on to write a children's story book entitled *The Adventures of Sherb and Pip* and brought all the characters to life through products such as bags, wash bags and soft toys. He talked to retailers and managed to get his products into over 60 UK stores. In 2016, Henry was a keynote speaker at the prestigious Retail Week Live event at the O2 in London. Since then he has been booked to speak at corporate events for brands such as Lego, the Company of Master Jewellers, Mumpreneur and Clarks. In January 2018, now 14, Henry set up Young & Mighty, an online space to inspire young people to turn their idea into a thing.

3. A bit about your business

You need to write a few lines describing your business and products. Here's what Henry says about his new venture Young & Mighty.

> *Young & Mighty is an online space where young people aged 11 to 14 years can find out about how to get cool jobs when they finish education. It also has a section on money-making and*

fundraising ideas, and a survival guide for some of the stuff life throws at you.

4. Finally you need to introduce yourself to your target list

This sounds straightforward but even PR agencies can get this bit wrong and it is very easy to annoy the editors and journalists.

Unless you have a huge breaking news story, always contact the press by email. It is much easier to say exactly what you need to say this way and they can look at it in their own time.

Always write to one journalist at a time. Don't send the same email to them all, as it won't be personal.

Here is an example:

> Dear Tom [use their name and make sure you spell it right!],
>
> I am 14 years old and make pictures out of recycled materials. I see that you write a column on young entrepreneurs and wonder if you would be interested in my story. I have been running my business, Second Glance, for 12 months and have created ten products. I attach some photos of my products and me in my studio to give you an idea of what I do.
>
> I look forward to hearing from you.
>
> [Your name]
>
> [Your website if you have one]

GETTING THE LOCAL PRESS INVOLVED IN YOUR EVENT

If you are holding an event – for example, a fundraising talent show – you can aim to get your local paper to write two articles:

1. They can write a news piece, hopefully a few weeks before the event, sharing the details: date, venue, time and how people can enter.

2. Then they can attend the event and write a report about what happened, how much money was raised and what a great success it was.

Email the news reporter two weeks before the date of the event, to give them plenty of time to plan the stories.

The email can be very simple. Here is an example.

> Dear Jane [if you know the name of the news reporter] or News Desk [if you don't],
>
> I am running a charity talent show at Buckingham Town Hall at 7pm on Friday 20 October.
>
> We are raising money to build a new playground at Greenacres School, Buckingham.
>
> I would like to invite you and your photographer to the event as it will be a popular date in the community calendar.
>
> Below is some further information on the event, if you are interested in writing a preview.
>
> The show is open to singers, actors, musicians, magicians, talented pets and dancers. If you have a talent or special trick come along and entertain the people of Buckingham.

The talent show has two sections – children and adults – and it costs £5 to enter.

Please email: [email address] or post your entry to [name and address].

Tickets for the show can be purchased at the door for £3 per person.

All the money raised will go towards the new playground.

Let me know if this is of interest.

Henry Patterson

A phone number [you must include a way for the reporter to contact you]

INTERVIEW TIPS

Henry will be the first to tell you about the importance of preparing for an interview. One of his first TV interviews was for CNBC and it was a disaster. He spent so long telling the presenter about what he did before setting up Not Before Tea that they ran out of time. He was mortified and will never make that mistake again.

Most interviews will be on the phone and so it is really easy to have your notes in front of you. Print out the paragraphs you wrote for your press library but now tell the story in your own voice. "I set up Second Glance because I was horrified by how much we throw away... etc."

It seems silly, but being interviewed can make you nervous and even a simple question like "What do you do?" might cause you to stumble. If possible,

ask the journalist to send over the questions they want to ask you beforehand. This will give you time to prepare.

If you don't have their questions, try to imagine what they are likely to ask. They will probably want to know what gave you the idea, who helped you and what you plan to do next.

Listen to the questions you're asked, speak clearly and try to keep your answers quite short. Let your personality shine through and remember you don't have to answer anything you don't want to.

CREATE YOUR OWN MARKETING PLAN

The final activity is for you to create a 12-month activity plan for your business (a starter template to help you is on page 188).

1. Turn a piece of A4 paper on its side and draw 12 columns.

2. Start with the month you are in and write the next 11 months across the top.

3. Then start filling all the columns with as many activities or events relevant to your business as you can. This will show you the quiet months that you might have to look harder for activities and will give you a really good idea of blog topics and video opportunities and so on.

Here are some ideas to help you fill the next 12 months:

★ Google national awareness days and see what fits you and your business. There are some crazy days like National Chocolate Day. These are great topics to cover on Instagram and blogs – but remember they need to be relevant to your business.

★ Write down all the events where you might want to have a stand. Maybe your school has a summer fete and you want to sell your T-shirts. Write it down and you can then plan when you have to start making your products to have them ready in time for the fete.

★ Write down the deadline for any awards you want to enter (just Google entrepreneur awards and you will find lots).

★ Write down events you want to attend to get the skills you need for your business. It might be a workshop on how to boost your followers on YouTube.

★ Is your product seasonal? If it is, write down the dates for Father's Day, Easter, Halloween, Christmas, Valentine's Day, Mother's Day, and back to school.

★ Write down other dates relevant to your business. Wimbledon for tennis, the start of the football season, country shows or carnivals.

★ There may be other important dates, such as your business's birthday, or dates when you plan to preview or launch a new product.

So you now have a list of the marketing tools you are going to use: a press library, a press list of publications and contact details, interview tips and a 12-month marketing plan. When you are ready to tell the world about your amazing business, you are going to smash it.

One last thing: notice I said when you are **ready** to tell the world? Don't start any activity until you are prepared. Have you got the stock you need? Is your website live?

Remember I told you about Henry getting 62,000 hits to his website in one morning? I didn't tell you that he had only made 32 jars of sweets. Another lesson learnt the hard way!

PROTECTING YOUR IDEAS

By Ian Zant-Boer,
Principal lawyer at leading law firm EMW

I am often asked for advice on how to protect an idea, piece of music, app or design. I thought it best to seek advice from one of the best lawyers I know, who also won't baffle us all with legal jargon.

Over to the very knowledgeable **Ian Zant-Boer** *to give us the lowdown...*

Perhaps you've come up with the next big app or have simply seen a demand in the market for a particular product. Either way, you will want to protect your idea and your fledgling business. Entrepreneurs have a number of options available to them to do this, including: copyright, trade marks and patents (pronounced pat-ent, not pay-tent). These rights are collectively referred to as **intellectual property**. But why is it important to obtain intellectual property protection?

These protections help to stop people stealing or copying the name of your product, your invention, the design and visual appearance of your product and anything you write, make or produce. Without these protections it is possible for someone else to benefit from your original idea and profit as a result.

COPYRIGHT

Copyright is an automatic right you receive when you have created a piece of work, such as writing, art, photography, films, music, web content and sound recordings (so long as you haven't copied someone else's original work).

Copyright stops others from copying your work, or changing it slightly and selling it as their own. You can mark your work with the © symbol, your name and the year the work was created to show your rights in the work. However, this does not affect the level of protection you have.

An easy way to establish the date you created your piece of work is to post a copy of it to yourself and then keep the UNOPENED envelope.

TRADE MARKS

You have to apply to register a trade mark and there are also fees (which can be quite expensive), so this will be more applicable to a business that has started to develop a customer base. Trade marks are used to protect your brand, such as your logo or business name. This is very important to a business as the recognition of a brand holds a lot of value. Most supermarkets sell their own-brand versions of food items at a lower price, which are often very similar in taste and yet we stick to the brands we know.

If we say baked beans, digestive biscuits and fish fingers, which brands do you think of? Put it to the test with your friends and family and you will see the power of the brand. In 2017 Apple was estimated to have the world's largest brand, valued at $170 billion.

PATENTS

Patents are used to protect inventions. They give the patent owner the exclusive right to control how their patented invention is used for a period of 20 years. They also give the patent owner the right to take legal action against someone who makes, uses or sells their invention without their permission.

To get a patent your invention will need to be:

★ something that can be made

★ new

★ inventive (so not just an obvious modification of someone else's invention).

Patents are the trickiest form of intellectual property to obtain and generally require expert advice which means they are also very expensive. However, where a genuine invention has been created they can be crucial. Sir Tim Berners-Lee invented the World Wide Web. However, he did not patent his creation and so the world was free to use his invention without having to pay him any money to do so. Luckily for us, Sir Tim actually *chose not to patent his invention* because he wanted it to be freely available. What a generous man!

SUMMARY

The intellectual property rights outlined above can often interlink. For example, a logo for a new business can be protected by copyright and can also be registered as a trade mark. This shows you how important intellectual property can be in enhancing the value of a business and its ideas.

If you want to know more about intellectual property visit: **www.gov.uk/government/organisations/intellectual-property-office**

GENERAL LEGAL ADVICE

Consumer law

When selling any products, consumer law will apply. It is important to be aware of some of the main responsibilities you as the seller will have and this will be increasingly important as your business grows. Depending on the goods you sell, a customer is entitled to:

★ an immediate refund if the goods are faulty (within 30 days of purchase)

★ a repair or replacement of the goods, but if they can't be repaired or replaced then the customer may be entitled to a refund (within six months of purchase)

★ if the goods do not last a reasonable length of time the customer may be entitled to some money back (up to six years after purchase!).

However, a customer does not have a legal right to a refund or replacement simply because they change their mind; the goods must be faulty.

This is a potentially important consideration for a business and how it manages income from customers. It may be helpful to the business's cash flow to set some money aside to cover the cost of any refunds or replacements that may be requested. It is also useful to understand the customer's rights to help maintain a good business image and brand.

It's not all about the law

Any business needs to be aware of the law and its rights. However, it must also consider the commercial implications in any business transaction. For example, let's imagine you run a tuck shop. A customer returns with a half-eaten cupcake complaining that he has decided he doesn't like the flavour and wants to swap it for another one. What do you do? You would probably tell the customer there is nothing you can do as the cupcake is perfectly fine but he is welcome to buy another. This is reasonable as it is not your fault that the customer doesn't like the flavour of his cupcake.

How would this scenario change if the customer had come to the tuck shop everyday for the last three months to buy a cupcake? You do not have to give him a free cupcake, but this is a long-standing customer and you may take the commercial decision that giving him a free replacement cupcake is better for the business in the long run to help ensure the customer returns for another three months.

Setting up with a friend

You may have had an idea with a friend, or think that involving a friend could be a useful way to grow your business. Unfortunately, friends and business do not always mix and the last thing you want is to lose one or the other.

As lawyers, we draft complex and detailed agreements to set out the relationship between our client and another party. The truth is that these agreements are rarely looked at while the parties get along and they will observe the terms and conditions in their day-to-day activities.

So what is the purpose of these agreements? They are put in place in case the parties fall out or disagree about what they said they would do. In this sense the agreement is a safety net that the parties can turn back to and see who is right.

While you may not want to use lawyers to draft a complex agreement, you should always put any agreement with a friend in writing. If there is any dispute you can look to the agreement to see what was agreed. Anything you put in writing should include:

★ what you are doing

★ what roles you are each taking on

★ how any money or other benefit is to be divided among you

★ what happens if something goes wrong.

This should help to minimise any disputes and, where they do still arise, ensure that the outcome is as originally intended between you.

LESSONS I HAVE LEARNT (OFTEN THE HARD WAY)

Hello, it's Henry again! I have learnt so much over the past few years. I have done some things quite by accident that have turned out brilliantly and I have made some really big mistakes which turned out terribly.

You know when you are at a boardroom table, talking to one of the biggest agents in the world, and your mother kicks you under the table, that things are not going well!

Here are my top eight pieces of advice to stop this from happening to you...

1. SOMETIMES YOU SIMPLY CAN'T PREPARE

One huge lesson I've learnt is that you simply can't prepare for everything. One day I had an exciting speaking slot in front of a large audience. The week before we had booked our train tickets. We'd left an hour early to make sure that we'd still make it if the trains were delayed. We had my presentation on about three memory sticks and made sure that everything that possibly could be planned was planned.

We arrived. All was going to plan. We were super early so my mum thought that it would be a great idea to go to a café. Big mistake. We were sat there happily with two bottles of water. As I leant over to put my headphones down, I caught one of the bottles – and the water went all over my trousers.

We looked at our watches: I was on stage ten minutes. These are the moments where teamwork is key and the only things that you can do are simply the only things you can do. Mum and I ran to the toilets but then realised that one of us was going to have to go in the other's toilets. After some persuasion I did eventually go into the women's loos and stood there embarrassed in a cubicle whilst my mother put my trousers under a hand dryer.

We had no warning that that was going to happen – it was just one of those things.

But on the bright side I learnt that you simply can't prepare for everything and that even when things do go wrong it will usually turn out OK.

2. REMOVE ALL DISTRACTIONS

Another thing I've learnt is to remove all distractions. This is something that I'd like to think I'm better at now but in reality that's probably not true.

In most meeting rooms, offices and – in some unfortunate cases – television studios they have spinning chairs. Now, let's be honest. Who doesn't love a spinning chair? There have been several occasions where I haven't been able to resist the temptation of giving myself a little spin around on these revolutionary furniture miracles.

Unfortunately, this has led to me being totally distracted while talking to someone. In one case I was told off by the CEO of a huge global supermarket.

Spinning chairs aren't the only distractions I've faced. Never use your iPad or laptop as a notebook – they are far too distracting. I once took some notes on my iPad when suddenly a couple of notifications came up one after another. I thought to myself: will it really hurt if I just check two? Yes. Yes it does.

Eventually I found myself in GarageBand playing the church organ.

My third and final distraction: me. Always remember, this may be the one chance that you've got to impress the person you're talking to. I have a habit of suddenly noticing something and only thinking about that when I should really be thinking of something else.

I once had a very important interview for a big agency and I just wasn't focusing. There wasn't a spinning chair and there wasn't a phone, tablet or laptop. I just kept thinking of different things, which eventually led to them saying 'no'.

You know what's going to distract you. Whether it's a spinning chair, or a computer or anything else, try to forget about it for now and stay focused.

3. BE YOURSELF

When I first started running my own business, I thought that I had to wear a suit to look professional. Now I realise that people can see through a suit. You don't need to pretend to be someone you're not.

I always felt very awkward in a suit. I felt like I was trying to be someone I wasn't. I

think people might have picked up on that – and even have felt uncomfortable themselves.

I went on *The One Show* (a British television chat show) in 2014 with Sir Richard Branson. I learnt that he feels the same. This doesn't mean that wearing a suit isn't being yourself. You may love wearing a suit and that's totally fine. But there is no point pretending to be someone that you're not – everyone will be able to tell that it's not the real you.

There's also no need to say or do anything that isn't what you would say or do.

My first ever photoshoot was in 2013. The photographer wanted me to look like a very serious businessman so he asked me to wear a pinstripe suit, to slick back my hair and pull a very straight face. No, before you ask, the photo will not be going in this book, only because I am 100% not paying for the rights to a photo that makes me look like Augustus Gloop.

Be clean and tidy but most of all – be yourself.

4. INTERVIEWS AND MEETINGS

Interviews and meetings are vital when you want to become an entrepreneur.

Everyone will have at least one meeting in their lives and I am pretty sure a few more on top. However, as great or as frightening as they may sound, there are a few vital things you need to know.

In 2015 I was invited onto *Saturday Live* on Radio 4. This was undoubtedly one of the strangest things that I've ever witnessed. Half way through my mother was asked to build an IKEA shelving unit. Live on the radio!

However, I've no tips for that.

The one tip I do have is to plan what you need to say. During the entire interview I chatted about everything and anything but didn't actually mention the name of my company or what it does. Not once. That meant that apart from having a really fun time, the interview didn't promote my business at all.

Another interview lesson takes me all the way back to 2013 when I was fresh out of my old school and Not Before Tea had just launched. I had been invited on the business network, CNBC. They asked me about my story, and me being me, I started from the very beginning.

No, really.

My opening sentence was, "I was born on January 15th 2004". So, when my airtime was up, I had only got as far as my seventh birthday.

That taught me to always have a few things up my sleeve. Like a script. Have the foundations of what you want to say really clear. For instance, if you had a cake business, your foundation might be:

> I started because my great grandad was a chef.
>
> *(Then you would talk about what he did and a bit more about the history.)*
>
> My parents bought me a baking kit.
>
> *(Then you might talk about what you did with the baking kit.)*
>
> Then I sold my cakes in my village.
>
> *(You could talk about how many you sold – or that you didn't sell any.)*

So you only need a couple of milestones to get your brain going and then you've got a story to tell.

5. POINT OUT YOUR QUIRKS

We all have quirks or blemishes. And pointing them out just makes life a whole lot better. Now this can come in two different forms. One is an icebreaker and the other is just to spot it before other people do.

People can be nasty about your quirks and it can be very hurtful. But if they have nothing to point out, they have nothing to say.

I'll start with the first point. I developed a stammer in 2013. That wasn't the best thing for someone who was sometimes asked to speak in public. When you see someone stammer on stage or get nervous it's so uncomfortable for the audience. This is why it's always good to have a little icebreaker at the beginning. At the beginning of most of my talks I always make a little joke about my stammer. Strangely, each time I do that I never stammer afterwards.

My second point is really important. When I was in lots of newspapers in 2013 I got a lot of nasty comments. Not from the press but from the readers – on forums, on social media. Some of them were really nasty personal comments.

However, I can't go on about them like I'm the only one – because we all get them. Whenever someone succeeds or does something amazing some people just get so jealous that they decide to write horrible things about you. And unfortunately they'll pick out all of your quirks and blemishes. For me it was my teeth, my hair or my weight.

Look, I'm not saying step outside and go and shout about how your hair looks as though several geese are trying to escape from a haystack, but just say, 'I know.'

The nasty remarks come from a tiny percentage of people who are eventually overpowered by the lovely, amazing, truly touching comments that you get. You just need to remember that out of the seven billion people on earth, at least one person will support you even if the other 6,999,999,999 people don't.

6. NEVER SHY AWAY FROM AN OPPORTUNITY

Life is full of opportunities and I've been fortunate enough to come across a couple myself. But some people can freak out and shy away from them. However, I've learnt not to. An opportunity is an opportunity.

In July 2015 my mother received an email asking me to speak at Retail Week Live. This was amazing. But then she got to the bottom of the email, where it said:

"Retail Week Live 2016, March, O2"

Then I had to open the window for air.

But the important thing is we took the opportunity. We didn't know what I would do or whether it would be OK but we just took a deep breath and said yes. **Accept it and then panic!**

Some of the biggest opportunities come from the smallest of things. I wasn't a speaker at the Great British Entrepreneur Awards 2013, but just going there led me to the Spring Fair, which led to me speaking at the Mumpreneur conference in 2014 and 2015, which then led to me speaking at trade shows, then Retail

Week Live, where I got invitations to speak at Lego, Clarks, Arvarto and CMJ. That eventually led to me speaking worldwide, and setting up my foundation, which got me here.

Never shy away from an opportunity!

7. NEVER FEEL PRESSURED BY OTHER PEOPLE'S SUCCESS

Everyone is so quick to judge you by the number of likes, follows and views you have and often use these measures to decide how well you are doing. Only the other day someone pointed out to me that another business had more views on YouTube than mine. They said it in a very negative way, as if I had failed and my products were not as good as the business with all the views.

I got caught up in the race for the blue tick and the hunt for as many followers as possible until one day I realised that it is not a contest I will ever win or want to win.

It is not good to spend each day focusing on what other people have, what they are doing and wishing it was you. Remember that photos are just a snapshot of people's lives. Just because they post a smiley photo of themselves on a huge shopping spree doesn't mean they are happy.

It is easy to buy likes, views and followers. You can generate a huge following if you offer people a prize or other incentive, but it doesn't make them friends, customers or true fans.

I am not saying don't be ambitious and competitive to be the best you can, I am just saying go at your own pace. Of course a business that has been going five years will have made more sales than one who has been trading six months. If you have just started vlogging, you are not going to have the same amount of interaction as Zoella, who has worked very hard for years to build her fan base.

Build a solid foundation around you of people that support and respect you. Don't cut corners or rush things. Be careful you are not letting your ego get in the way. Think back to the story of the three little pigs: the brick house was the only one that stayed up. The ones built quickly, from straw and sticks, fell down at the first sign of trouble.

8. NEVER FORGET TO THANK PEOPLE WHO HELP

So many people say that they're going to do things but never actually do it. I have lost count of how many people say they will help or introduce me to someone and I never hear from them again. However, I've also been fortunate enough to meet a couple of exceptions to the rule. The one thing I've learnt from this is always to thank those who help me.

A great example of this is Michael Acton Smith, founder and CEO of Mind Candy, the company responsible for Moshi Monsters and World of Warriors.

He invited me to come and meet and interview him in 2014. He said that he would put me in touch with a lady who worked for a big newspaper and that's exactly what he did.

That newspaper changed my life, giving me so many opportunities, and I couldn't thank him enough.

I remembered that he told me his favourite food was key lime pie. So I sent him one the next day.

The importance of thanking people is huge. You've no idea how much even a card means to someone.

In 2017 my friend T'nnox and I used to travel to school together on the train. We used to pop into Starbucks on a daily basis, usually just to say hi. The Bedford Starbucks team were some of the nicest people that we'd ever met. All 12 of them!

In April we decided that we'd bring them chocolates, flowers and a card to say thanks and it was totally worth it. In fact, the local papers found out about our gifts and ran a story about their outstanding customer service. The whole team were so proud.

So whether you get in a newspaper or have your day brightened by Ryan and the Starbucks crew, it's so important to say thank you.

WITH A LITTLE HELP FROM MY FRIENDS

Ten things my pug Martha has taught me about being a successful entrepreneur

1. Never let go

When Martha has a stick, she will not let it go. She has put so much effort in to chasing it that when she finally gets it she holds on to it tightly. When I get an opportunity, I will make sure that I don't let it slip through my fingers and will see it through to the end.

2. Be persistent

It's not her best feature, but if Martha loses her toy down the back of the sofa, she will dig and scratch and dig and scratch for hours, until finally she finds her toy – or we get sick of her scratching and get it for her. Now I am not saying I scratch at the doors of potential customers and partners, but if I have a goal I will find a way to achieve it.

3. Be alert

Martha can be fast asleep and then hear a
noise and leap up instantly. I am always
amazed at how alert she is. I am learning to
do this in business. If you stay asleep or get
lazy, your competitor will overtake in a shot.

4. Be friendly

Martha gives every single person she meets
such a wonderful greeting. I always try to go over to people and
introduce myself and find out more about them. (I try not to
jump up, though!)

5. Have a good memory

Martha can bury a bone for months and then remember exactly
where it is and one day go and dig it up. I am pleased that I have
a good memory to remember names and to do what I promise to
do in meetings. I write everything down too.

6. Always be prepared

Whenever we pick up the lead, Martha is ready to go out. She is
always clean and presentable and ready to meet anyone. I have
been at events as a guest and then invited on stage to speak with
no notice at all. So a stained old T-shirt is OK to wear at home,
but if you're going out, think again!

7. Be adaptable

Sometimes I will walk Martha at 7 am, sometimes at 1 pm. She
is happy whenever it's time to go out. I can plan my week and

then something comes along that is too good to miss and I have to change my plans. Maybe I have to give up my day off or a lie in, but there are always other times for them. The opportunity might only ever appear once.

8. Be happy

Martha's tail is always spinning (pugs' tails don't wag, they spin). I don't always feel like chatting and my mother says I can be really moody sometimes, but I can't let it affect the rest of the team, my customers or people who book me to speak. I think this has been my hardest challenge. You have to leave your stress and moods at home and always give 100%.

9. Know when to stop

Martha is very good on her walks and is allowed off the lead when we get to an open space. At the end of the track where we walk there is a road and she knows to stop a little way before. I get very enthusiastic when I have new ideas and don't like it if people don't share my excitement or disagree with me. I have ignored other people's opinions and then been surprised when the products don't sell. You mustn't be afraid to stop and re-think your idea if it is not working.

10. Be ready to lead the way

Martha the pug will boldly run ahead and carve out tracks in the long grass, treading where no pug has trodden before. None of us must just follow others because it is the easiest and safest route. The world would be so boring if we all did that.

Five things my cat Hobbit has taught me about starting a business

1. Be patient

Hobbit has endless patience. She will crouch down and stay dead still for hours, waiting for a mouse to appear from a hole. Nothing will distract her. Starting a business can be a slow process as you have to get it right. I am so impatient and have realised that sometimes you just have to wait.

2. Pounce

See an idea or opportunity – pounce. That's what Hobbit does.

3. late nights and long days

Hobbit can go on extremely long adventures. She can be away for days at a time but then return and sleep for an entire day. My longest days are events and trade shows. I have much better stamina now and if I know I have some really long days ahead we make sure we put some duvet days in the diary too. Just like Hobbit.

4. Being alone

Hobbit spends most of her time alone. She will go into the village to meet up with other cats (at least I think she does) but most of the time she is on her own. When you first start a business, you do spend lots of time by yourself. Don't worry – it won't last forever – but warn your friends that they might not see much of you while you are getting set up. It is better to tell them upfront, so they don't think you have suddenly become the most antisocial person in the world.

5. Think outside the box

Hobbit takes this literally. She sleeps in the strangest of places: in cupboards, on top of a wobbly stack of boxes or a pile of dirty washing in the laundry basket. We are all different and we must celebrate that. I was told off at school for thinking differently, but I wouldn't have got very far thinking like everyone else.

PHOTO ALBUM

The first ever print run of my storybook Pip Gets a Job.

Book signing in my first stockist, Bentalls, Kingston, with my amazing illustrator Becky Down.

The first time I ever spoke on stage.

It is so amazing seeing your products for sale in a shop.

My wonderful shop.

Meeting Sir Richard Branson for the first time (and signing a copy of my book for him!)

Bird's eye view of the photo that will haunt me forever.

Filming The One Show.

Speaking at a Success Resources event in Asia for the first time.

PART FOUR: scribble and scribe

THE BIG PICTURE

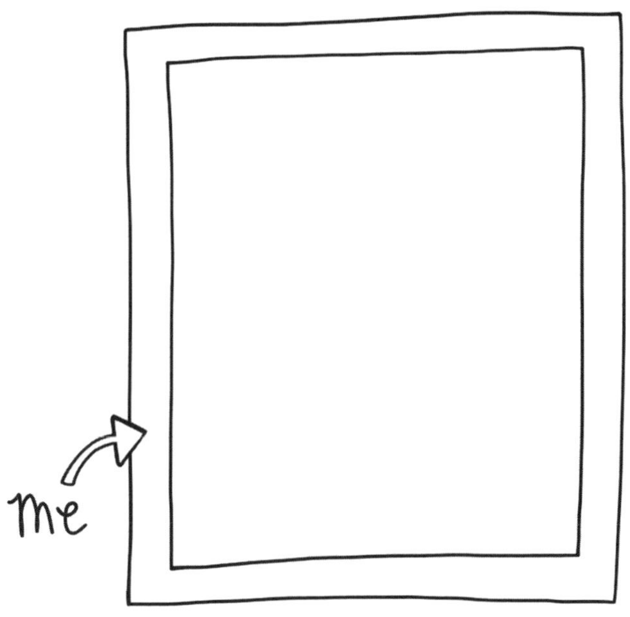

SELF PORTRAIT OF..

DRAW **3** PEOPLE WHO INSPIRE YOU AND WRITE WHY...

BIG
WAYS MY
GENERATION
CAN CHANGE
THE WORLD

SMALL WAYS I
CAN CHANGE THE
WORLD

ME IN 10 YEARS

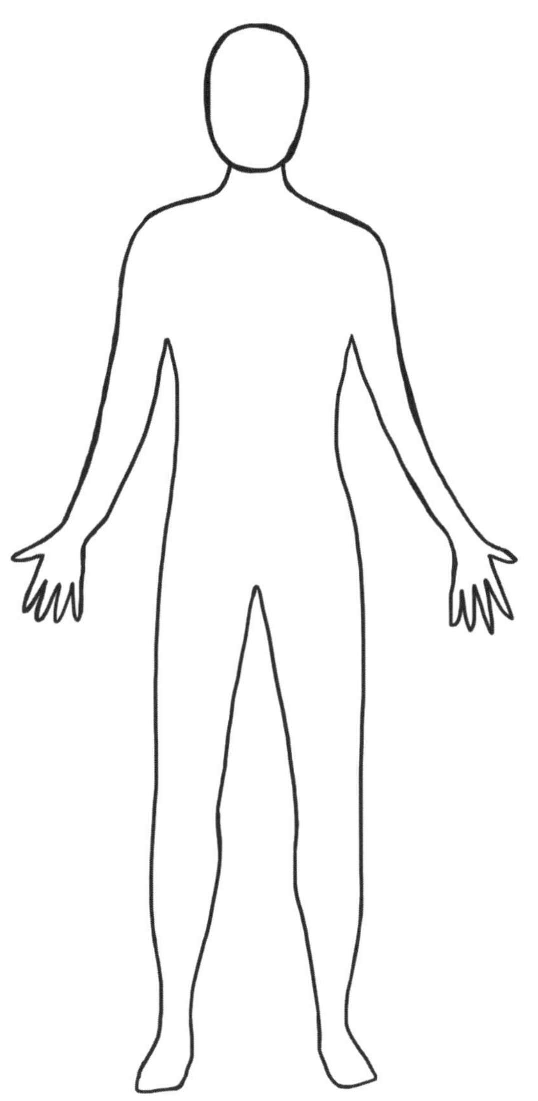

10 THINGS I WOULD LOVE TO ACHIEVE IN MY LIFE

1

2

3

4

5

6

7

8

9

10

IN 10 YEARS TIME I WOULD LOVE MY JOB TO BE...

I WANT TO SPEND MY DAYS DOING...

(Remember we spend over <u>57%</u> of our life working so it is so important we love what we do.)

ALL ABOUT
ME

GET SIGNING...

WHETHER YOU NEED TO PERFECT YOUR AUTOGRAPH FOR SIGNING BOOKS, OR A CLEAR SIGNATURE FOR YOUR BUSINESS DOCUMENTS, PRACTICE MAKES PERFECT.

PLAY AROUND WITH DIFFERENT VARIANTS OF YOUR NAME. WHICH FELT EASY AND NATURAL? AND THE BIG QUESTION — CAN YOU REPEAT IT OVER AND OVER AGAIN?

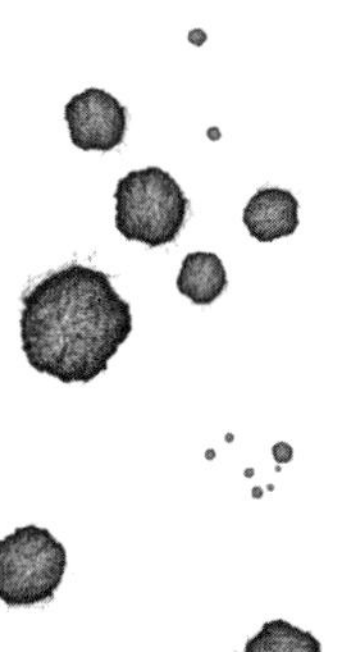

DESIGN YOUR FIRST BUSINESS CARD BELOW

FRONT

BACK

THE BEST ADVICE I HAVE EVER RECEIVED

ADVICE I IGNORED BUT SHOULD HAVE TAKEN

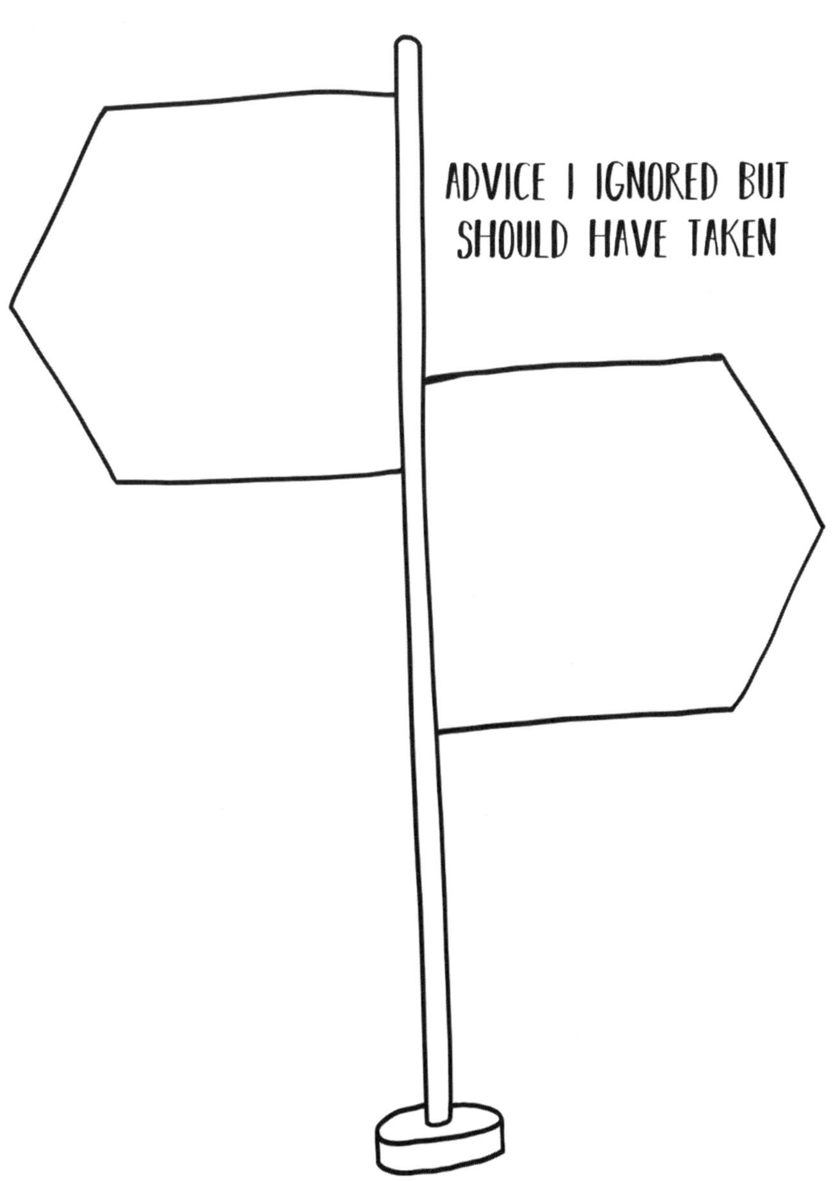

lovely things people have said about me...

Negative things people have said about me...

What can I learn from them?

PEN TO PAPER
LET'S PLAN!

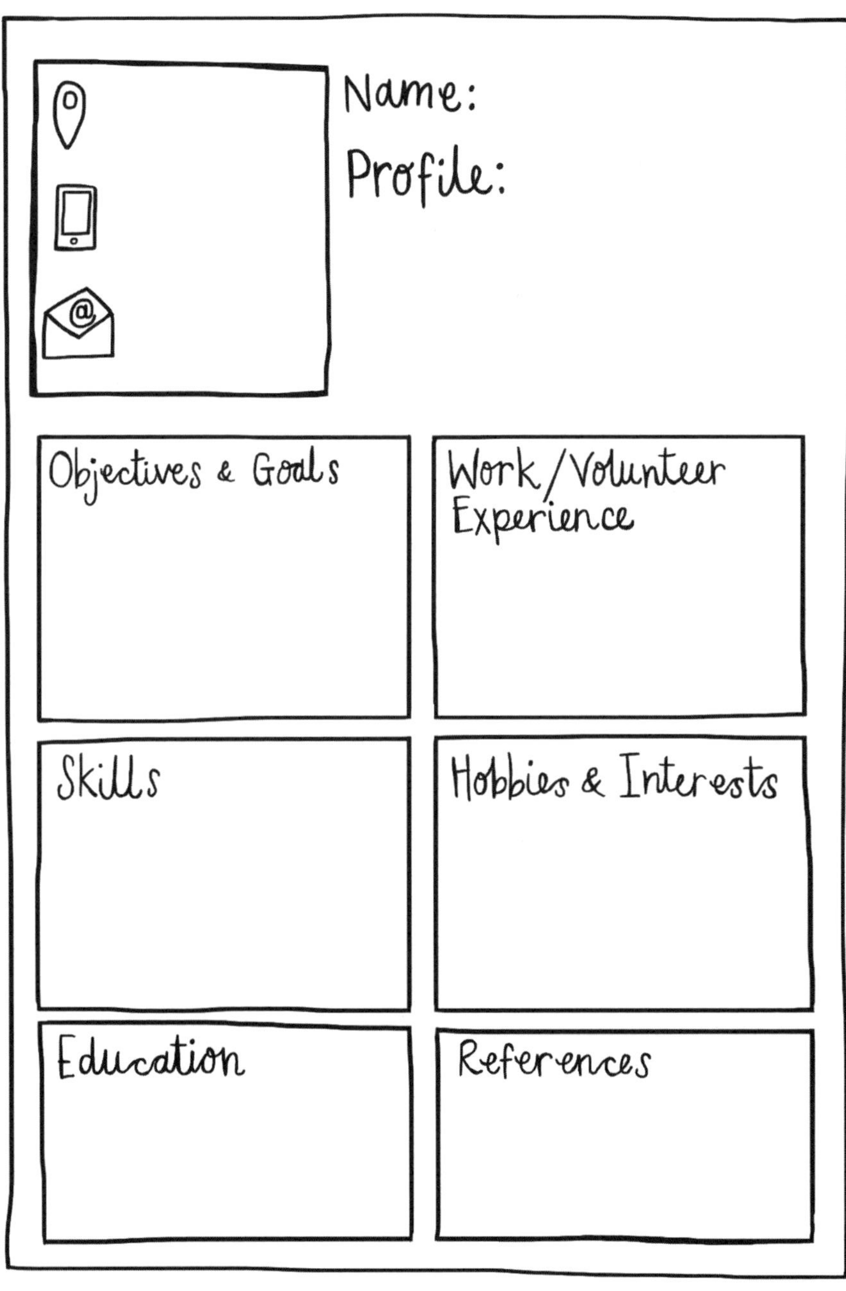

MY CV
Name:
Profile:
Objectives & Goals
Work/Volunteer Experience
Skills
Hobbies & Interests
Education
References

WHY?

____

____

____

WHAT CHARITY/ORGANISATION
ARE YOU FUNDING IN AID OF?

____

____

____

HOW CAN PEOPLE DONATE?
E.G. A BUCKET, SPONSORSHIP
FORM, JUSTGIVING PAGE ETC?

____

____

____

WHERE IS IT TAKING
PLACE?

____

____

____

MY FUNDRAISING IDEA IS...

____

WHO IS DOING IT?

____

____

____

WHAT IS THE TARGET
YOU WOULD LIKE TO RAISE?

____

____

____

HOW WILL YOU PROMOTE YOUR
FUNDRAISING? E.G. POSTERS,
FLYERS, FACEBOOK PAGE?

____

____

____

WHAT ARE YOUR
EXPENSES?

____

____

TARGET TRACKER

MY TARGET IS £...............

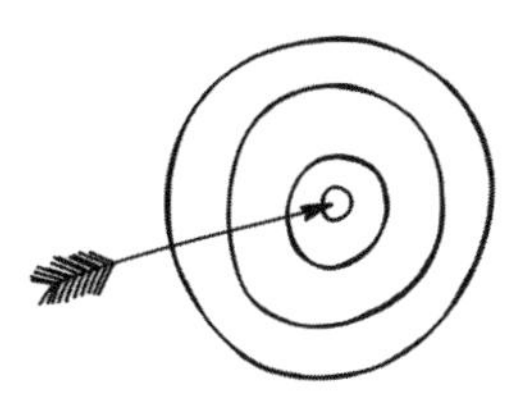

£200
£190
£180
£170
£160
£150
£140
£130
£120
£110
£100
£90
£80
£70
£60
£50
£40
£30
£20
£10

SHADE IN THE BOX AS YOU GET CLOSER TO REACHING YOUR TARGET

WHY?

WHAT CHARITY/ORGANISATION ARE YOU FUNDING IN AID OF?

HOW CAN PEOPLE DONATE? E.G. A BUCKET, SPONSORSHIP FORM, JUSTGIVING PAGE ETC?

WHERE IS IT TAKING PLACE?

MY FUNDRAISING IDEA IS...

WHO IS DOING IT?

WHAT IS THE TARGET YOU WOULD LIKE TO RAISE?

HOW WILL YOU PROMOTE YOUR FUNDRAISING? E.G. POSTERS, FLYERS, FACEBOOK PAGE?

WHAT ARE YOUR EXPENSES?

DONATIONS

TARGET TRACKER

MY TARGET IS £...............

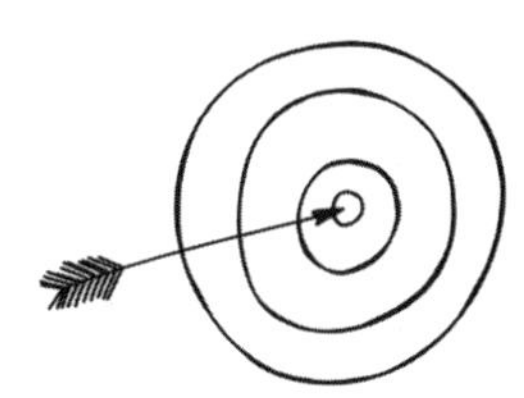

£200
£190
£180
£170
£160
£150
£140
£130
£120
£110
£100
£90
£80
£70
£60
£50
£40
£30
£20
£10

SHADE IN THE BOX AS YOU GET CLOSER TO REACHING YOUR TARGET

MY LITTLE BLACK BOOK

WHEN YOU START OUT IN BUSINESS, IT HELPS TO TURN TO FRIENDS AND FAMILY FOR SUPPORT.

BELOW IS A LIST OF SKILLS YOU MIGHT NEED. JOT DOWN WHO MIGHT BE SUITABLE FOR THAT ROLE:

★ Graphic Designer ....

★ Photographer ....

★ Web Designer ....

★ Accounting & Finance ....

★ Creative Maker ....

★ Writer ....

★ Sales - who can help you at events? ....

★ Social Media ....

★ Technical Support ....

★ Press Office ....

★ Marketing ....

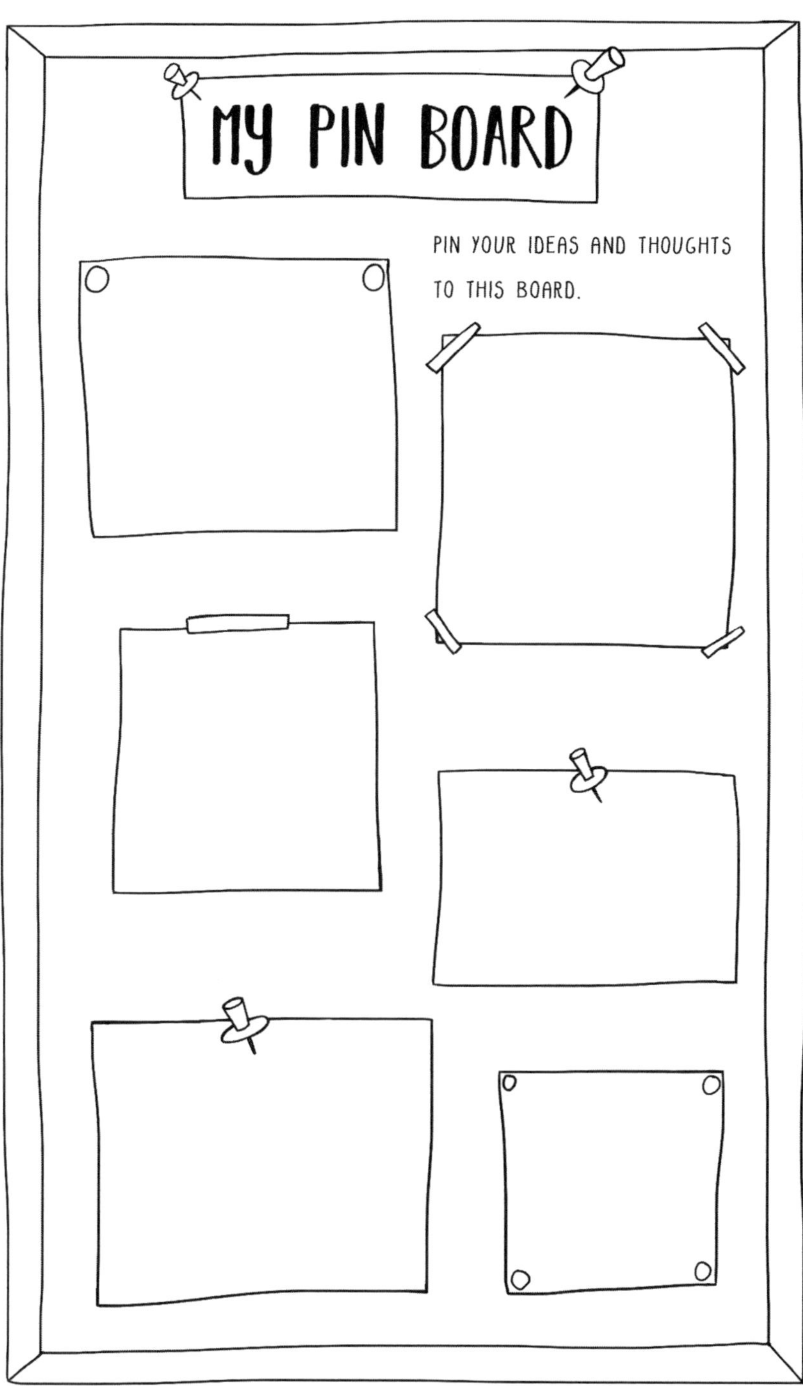

MY PIN BOARD
PIN YOUR IDEAS AND THOUGHTS TO THIS BOARD.

MY BUDGET PLANNER – Setting up my NEW business

SET UP COSTS – THINGS I NEED TO PAY FOR TO SET UP MY BUSINESS (STOCK, PRINTING, DESIGN ETC)

-
-
-
-
-
-
-
-
-
-

Total set-up costs: £..............

(HOW MUCH YOU NEED TO GET STARTED. SEE PART ONE FOR IDEAS ON HOW TO RAISE THIS AMOUNT.)

MY MONTHLY BUDGET

EXPENSES MONEY GOING OUT	COST	INCOME MONEY COMING IN	COST
TOTAL:		TOTAL:	

MY MARKETING PLAN

MONTH	ACTIVITY	TARGETS & GOALS
1		
2		
3		
4		
5		
6		
7		
8		
9		
10		
11		
12		

PART FIVE:
Learn from the Best

For this part of the book I asked some of my heroes to tell us a bit about how they got started in their careers and what advice they would pass on to their younger selves. I'm so grateful and humbled that they all agreed to be part of this book. They are listed in alphabetical order because every one of them is brilliant and I wouldn't dare organise it any other way.

NIGEL BOTTERILL

Entrepreneur, founder of nine separate million-pound-plus businesses and Entrepreneurs' Circle

When you were younger, how did you earn some money?

My dad used to come home from work every Thursday with a copy of *Shoot!* magazine and a £1 note for me. (This was before we had £1 coins!) Thursdays were special. *Shoot!* magazine, a one pound note and fish pie. My mum always made fish pie on a Thursday.

What advice would you give your younger self?

Three things:

1. Who you hang around with matters. A lot.

2. The only time success comes before work is in the dictionary.

3. If you want to be super successful you can't be like everyone else. And that's OK, because most people are not super successful.

What's one fun fact about yourself or your business?

Business owners that join Entrepreneurs Circle are more than twice as likely to build a million-pound business than those that don't.

If you were given £10, how would you double it in just five days?

I'd use it to buy a bucket, a sponge and a chamois leather and I'd set up a car-cleaning business. I'd go to a local business park and I'd clean cars.

SIR RICHARD BRANSON
Founder of the Virgin Group

When you were younger, how did you earn some money?

Growing up I learnt the value of money quickly. When I was younger my Auntie Joyce bet me 10 shillings (about 50p in today's money!) that I couldn't learn to swim by the end of our holiday. We were driving home from the holiday when I made the family pull over so I could have one last attempt at swimming in a river we were driving past. I was determined to win that 10 shillings but also learn how to swim.

Despite nearly drowning, I managed it. I'd never had that amount of money before and it was a great feeling but what was more rewarding was the fact I could now swim – it taught me a really important lesson: to not just find rewards which are monetary, but also ones which make you happy.

What advice would you give your younger self?

I would say: Ricky, your imagination is your greatest gift, never stop dreaming and creating – as you grow older you'll realise it's one of your strongest attributes. I would tell him it's important to not let the challenges and failures in life discourage you, as they teach us the greatest lessons.

And that while you may get into trouble sometimes, your parents will always have your best interests at heart. Be nice to your family and listen to your mum and dad – they will guide you through life and be there for you at every turn.

As you grow older you will realise just how important it is to do what you love and love what you do.

What's one fun fact about yourself or your business?

Although I've never been ashamed of talking about it, some people are perhaps not aware that I'm actually dyslexic. I struggled with it at school, long before it was widely known – my teachers just thought I was stupid or lazy. I think education has come a long way in its understanding of dyslexia, but we need to help those who are dealing with it as they often excel in many other areas like creativity – I've actually used it to my advantage in my business life. It's important to be confident in putting your hand up for the tasks which play to your strengths. Don't be afraid to be honest and ask for help on the ones which you find a little more challenging.

If you were given £10, how would you double it in just five days?

I would find something I loved doing or find something I'd love to change.

Whatever I've done in business has either been from a point of passion or a point of frustration. I need to believe in the industry and where it's heading. Frustration that a certain sector has grown complacent in what it offers customers.

The growth of companies like Uber or Airbnb show 'the sharing economy' is on the rise. More and more people are looking for ways to share the properties, cars and items they own with other people for a fee.

I would find something somebody wanted of mine and use my £10 to advertise its availability to rent, with the hope that would quickly grow! In fact, one of my favourite campaigns is Virgin Money's 'Make £5 Grow' challenge. It gives young people between 9 and 11 years old experience of starting a small business using a £5 loan from Virgin Money. It's in its sixth year and over 40,000 pupils have taken part – it's a brilliant way of inspiring future entrepreneurs.

ARIANA DEBOSE

Triple threat performer (singing, dancing and acting in musicals)

Original Broadway Cast of HAMILTON, A BRONX TALE, MOTOWN THE MUSICAL, and BRING IT ON: THE MUSICAL

Photo credit: Jocelyn Bold

When you were younger, how did you earn some money?

I worked behind the desk at my dance studio and I also sold lollipops for a dollar at school – they'd cost me 50 cents to buy a piece so I made a 50 cents profit. (Not sure how I got away with that, but I did.)

What advice would you give your younger self?

Stay curious. Learn as many skills as you possibly can. You should've really learned a few more real-world tricks. (I'm still no good at riding a bike or skateboarding and you'd be surprised how often things like that come up in my profession.)

What's one fun fact about yourself or your business?

I play dress up for a living and get paid pretty well to do it! Plus I get to meet some really amazing people on the daily, which helps keep me inspired. I also technically have free ice cream for life from Cold Stone Creamery. So the moral of the story is enter a lot of contests – you can win cool free things!

If you were given £10, how would you double it in just five days?

I'd probably sell lollipops again, but hire people to sell them for me at a higher price and cut them in on the profits... or I'd go sing in the subways. You'd be shocked how generous people can be when you just start singing to spread a little joy and happiness for no reason at all. In America we call it SHOWTIME!

LAVINIA DRAKE
Founder of Baking Time Club

When you were younger, how did you earn some money?

I had to do chores to get pocket money. I'd iron tea towels, wash the car and mow the lawn and any other odd jobs around the house. My mum worked for a drinks brand, so I spent my weekends at shows like BBC *Good Food Show*, when other companies were short staffed I'd help out as 'work experience' and spent a weekend selling cakes and chocolates. The best part was getting to take home a goodie bag of chocolate!

What advice would you give your younger self?

Don't worry about trying to be cool, being different is the best type of cool.

What's one fun fact about yourself or your business?

I create mixes of cake sprinkles for bakers and name them things like: Cosmic Blush, Mermaid's Tail and Rainbows for Days – yes, that's actually part of my job!

If you were given £10, how would you double it in just five days?

I'd bake a batch of cupcakes and sell them to hungry office workers.

FAYE MICHEL JARY
Wardrobe mistress for the West End

When you were younger, how did you earn some money?

I babysat, taught gymnastics and did chores for my parents.

What advice would you give your younger self?

Don't stress about exams so much. Just do your revision, do your best and you'll be fine. Also save your money from a young age, you won't regret it.

What's one fun fact about yourself or your business?

I work on such a variety of shows, of different time periods and styles of costumes, and I get to work with some incredible and fanciful costumes, and trying these on from time to time is definitely fun! We had some amazing hats on *Half a Sixpence* – huge, feathered, Ascot 1900's hats, they were screaming out to be worn!

If you were given £10, how would you double it in just five days?

Buying some tulle and making baby tulle tutus to sell, or felt and making up some Christmas tree decorations to sell. Easy, quick and fun!

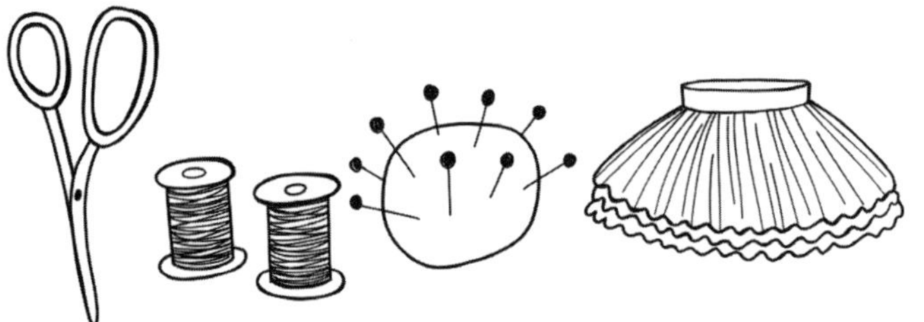

MIKE KRIEGER

Co-founder, Instagram

When you were younger, how did you earn some money?

A friend and I started a web design/web engineering business together. Keep in mind that this was around 1996, so there weren't as many designers and engineers doing website work back then. It was a fun way to turn the things we were interested in – making websites, learning to code – into something a little bigger.

What advice would you give your younger self?

Don't be limited to geographic boundaries. The world is your community.

What's one fun fact about yourself or your business?

The 'Juno' filter in Instagram is named after my dog, Juno.

If you were given £10, how would you double it in just five days?

As I'm writing this, it's about to be the July 4th holiday here in the United States and there's a heatwave. So perhaps I would turn those £10 into a few reusable water bottles that people might want to buy at an event.

SIR CAMERON MACKINTOSH
Theatre producer

When you were younger, how did you earn some money?

As I was at boarding school in my early teens and there was still an element of postwar rationing in place, there was very little money about so I survived on small handouts from my parents and aunts. It was actually my aunts that were the keenest theatregoers, so they regularly treated me to see the latest West End hits, including the musical *Salad Days* which inspired my career. During school holidays, I worked part time in a local factory, folding cardboard packing cases (urgh!) and also had the odd job working in the family timber company near my home.

What advice would you give your younger self?

The best advice I ever read when I was young was, "In choosing a project, do it because you love it, not just to make money – if you do it as well as you can, then hopefully the public will like it too." I also discovered – when starting out my career and living on a pittance – that whatever job you managed to get, if you did it well and made yourself indispensable, people would notice and you usually got offered something far more exciting and interesting which would open new doors.

What's one fun fact about yourself or your business?

One of the most interesting observations about me was written by Stephen Sondheim when he said that "Cameron makes commerce out of art, not art out of commerce". I've never been interested in making money for its own sake, only making enough money to continue to be able to choose which show I would do next. I have never quantified success.

If you were given £10, how would you double it in just five days?

I haven't a clue how to double my money quickly, because I'm not an entrepreneur, just a producer! All my best investments have come about from doing what I love – so if I was given £10, I would probably give it to someone else to whom the money would mean double what it means to me.

NATASHA MINTER

International model (including John Frieda TV commercial, L'Oréal campaign and London Fashion Week)

When you were younger, how did you earn some money?

Ironing! I did the ironing from the age of 11 onwards.

What advice would you give your younger self?

Don't hang out with mean girls. Be kinder to your family. Don't hold grudges.

What's one fun fact about yourself or your business?

My business is called Model Me – it has nothing to do with modelling but everything to do with being a role model. Model Me is all about empowerment – through two ways, the first being through our health programme, The Train Eat Think Program, focusing on fitness, nutrition and mindset. I really believe that in order to live an all-round healthy life you need to focus on all three pillars. It's not about changing everything – just making a small change in each section of your life can make a MASSIVE impact on your whole life.

If you were given £10, how would you double it in just five days?

I would buy a range of fresh fruit and make smoothies and fruit salads. I would then head to a business park and call on the offices and sell them as a great afternoon snack. I would at least triple my money and also give people their five-a-day – it's a win-win!

THEO PAPHITIS
Shopkeeper

When you were younger, how did you earn some money?

Money was extremely tight when I was younger and we really had to fend for ourselves. I had a variety of jobs, but a great one was delivering cards for a local minicab company in London. I was 12 and it was my first experience of direct marketing. The first time I did it, it was a test, though I didn't know that at the time. The cab owner wanted to check I wasn't just dumping them in a bin, but the fact that he received calls from them meant I had a job for a few years – it was a lesson for me in doing a job properly! I loved walking so I enjoyed the work, and earned as much as £3 or £4 a go. It meant I didn't have to bother my mum for money and was able to buy myself clothes and things I needed, as well as start to save money. It was my first step into financial independence and it felt good.

What advice would you give your younger self?

Keep dreaming and never doubt those dreams. Dreams are where it all begins and you have to believe that you can make them come true, as you're the only person who can do that. I often say the harder I work, the luckier I get, and it is so true because nothing ever fell into my lap. I dreamt of a better life, and I worked very hard to make it a reality. Realising dreams is about having a passion and if you work hard, anything is possible.

What's one fun fact about yourself or your business?

A key turning point for me in my life was answering a job advert that Mrs P had seen in the local paper, as a sales person for Tyme, part of Watches of Switzerland in Bond Street. Finding that job advert, having that interview and getting the job kick-started my passion for retail, sales and people. I was lucky to find my passion early and I still have that love of retail today. It's important to do what you love as you'll be doing it a long time. I'm a nostalgic person, and I carried that job advert, a cutting from a paper, around with me for about 20 years afterwards. It is a precious piece of my history. I still have it at home today and would never throw it away! Keep an eye out for those magical windows of opportunity and grab them with both hands.

If you were given £10, how would you double it in just five days?

As it's such a short amount of time to turn around a profit, it would definitely have to be something seasonal and reactive. I'd quickly do my homework on identifying the 'who, what, when, where and why' of the marketplace to make the most of my selling window. To more than double money in just five days, my product could perhaps be fans or umbrellas to deal with extremes in the weather. You have to always keep an eye on what people need and when, and be able to respond quickly, especially if you're after a quick profit.

LAURA PHELAN

Eating disorder specialist, therapist and speaker

When you were younger, how did you earn some money?

From what I can remember, my mum would always provide me with what I needed, I don't remember getting 'fixed' pocket money. Maybe I got £5 for the days I wanted to eat lunch at school or go to the cinema, as it used to be that cheap back in the day! I would have also used birthday money to put towards things I wanted to do or buy.

What advice would you give your younger self?

I wish I had taken a little more interest in money back then, I guess. I always struggled with maths so it put me off thinking about it at all and that led to me having no real idea about how to budget in my teens.

What's one fun fact about yourself or your business?

I set up my own organisation (Phelan Well) after my own recovery from an eating disorder, which started as mentoring in and outside schools. Appearances in the media led me to specialise in this area, and I now help people one-to-one, speak all over the country and run my own events to help people develop a healthier relationship with themselves and food.

If you were given £10, how would you double it in just five days?

For 13-year-old dog-loving me, I would print some posters and leaflets for my local area offering dog walking for £5 per dog. I would make £20 by walking just four dogs and I would have so much fun doing it!

TIM STOCKDALE
International showjumper

When you were younger, how did you earn some money?

I used to sell eggs. I rescued some old battery hens and sold their eggs once they had started to lay again. I would also buy old clothes from charity shops and resell them to friends who were into mod fashion that was coming in at that time. I would restore old bikes and sell them. We had horse chestnut trees and I would collect the conkers, get them ready to play with and sell bags of them to school friends (until the school banned conker fights because of the mess).

What advice would you give your younger self?

School grades don't matter. People invest in people not their grades.

What's one fun fact about yourself or your business?

I had to run out of the bank once so they couldn't take my cheque book from me. I had slight cash flow problems!

If you were given £10, how would you double it in just five days?

Get some flyers printed off with the money and offer my services to dog walk, tidy gardens, clean windows, generally any jobs around the village. £10 per hour, easy!

CHRISTOPHER TENDAI

Choreographer, teacher and performer (performer credits include: Hamilton Original London Cast, Jesus Christ Superstar and In The Heights)

Photo credit: Sam Mackay

When you were younger, how did you earn some money?

When I was 11–14 I got £10 pocket money from my dad and also sold sweets at school!

What advice would you give your younger self?

I would tell my younger self to have more fun and to not care about what other people think of me.

What's one fun fact about yourself or your business?

Whenever I go on for one of my swing tracks for the first time, apparently my eyes always widen to double the size as I'm trying to find out where I'm going! I am now known as Wide Eyes from all of the shows I've been in.

If you were given £10, how would you double it in just five days?

If I was given £10 tomorrow, I would (as a teacher) hire a small studio space for an hour and hold a private lesson with a student. Or I would buy ingredients to bake three big cakes. I would then sell slices of the cake at a certain price.

HOLLY TUCKER

Co-founder of Notonthehighstreet.com and founder of
Holly & Co

When you were younger, how did you earn some money?

I knew from a very young age that I wanted to run my own business – I started my school's first tuck shop aged 13. My first 'proper' job was a year later when my dad would drop me at 6 am at a pub, where I was the weekend cleaner, and he'd wait parked in the pub car park until I was finished.

What advice would you give your younger self?

Trust your gut instinct. People will be very quick to offer advice (whether you ask for it or not), but listening carefully to your own instincts is crucial to survive in business. It certainly isn't an easy thing to do, but once you learn to listen to yourself, your inner compass will guide you in the right direction

What's one fun fact about yourself or your business?

I have a (not so secret!) addiction to Monster Munch crisps – I LOVE THEM!

If you were given £10, how would you double it in just five days?

This is a tough question! It would have to be something I really believe in and am passionate about – there's no point going into business with anything (even if only for five days) if you don't love it, because then you won't be able to convincingly sell it. Most likely, I would find a product I loved and put it on my Instagram page and across social media. It's free marketing and if it's a good product that people like and is photographed well, your customers will do the work of selling for you by putting your product on their social media pages!

SARAH WILLINGHAM
Entrepreneur/investor

When you were younger, how did you earn some money?

I earned money from the age of 11. I started delivering papers and then swept the hair in the local hairdressers. At the age of 13 I worked as a waitress.

What advice would you give your younger self?

Be kind, leave more than you take, eat well and exercise. Believe, believe, believe in yourself. It is your path, carve it out, make your way, live the life you want to live. You do not ever need to follow the crowd – be strong.

What's one fun fact about yourself or your business?

Staffordshire oatcakes are still my favourite food in the whole world.

If you were given £10, how would you double it in just five days?

Buy a vintage dress/bag/shoes from a charity shop and sell it on eBay.

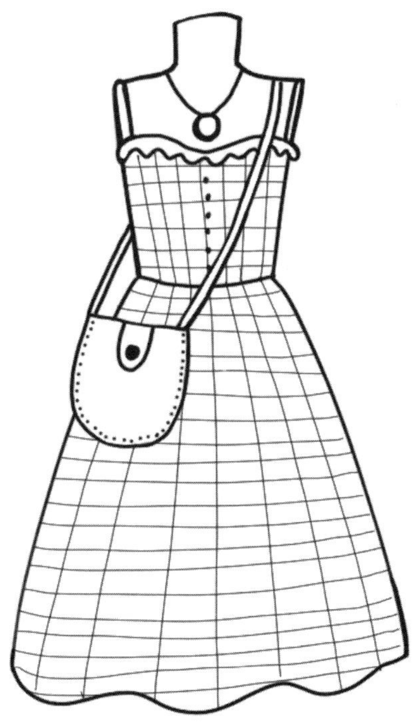

Final Word

So that's the end of this book and one thing's for certain: you and I have a real adventure ahead of us.

People often say that our younger years are the best and it definitely doesn't feel like that sometimes, but there must be some truth in it.

It's fun exploring and finding out what you want to do in life. We are the next generation and will make mistakes, but we will also have triumphs and make something of our lives.

Hamilton has a line that couldn't be more true: *history has its eyes on you.*

We're all on a road, with so many different ways to go. No one can ever say that this is the only way to go. Nor will your road always be clear and obvious.

You are going to hit a red light, have to make a U-turn, turn left, turn right, take the second exit, stop at a service station to get a quick iced caramel macchiato (that would be my path!) and be held up by roadworks along the way.

But in the end it's your motivation and inspiration that will fuel your journey.

It's our job to write our story, the pen is in your hands.

Let's do this!

Henry X

This was me, straight after I had written the last word of this book. I had to take it on holiday as I had not quite finished and this photo captures the amazing feeling of achievement when I had written my 25,000th word! Never forget to give yourself a pat on the back and celebrate how far you have come.

Thank you

There are so many people I want to thank but must of course start with my family. Thanks to all of you for being so supportive and helping me make all of this possible.

I want to say a special thank you to my wonderful Grandma Pet, who sadly died whilst I was writing this book. She would have loved to see it finished.

Thanks to Tommii and Harriet for not only helping with Young & Mighty but for being great friends.

To Mark Brewer, Rachel Baade, Buzby Allen and the rest of the team at Potters for making me laugh until I cry and given me great opportunities on their stage.

Huge thanks to Ralph Allwood, Martyn Ford and everyone at the Junior Choral Course for giving me the best weeks of my life and helping me find my passion.

Thanks to Harriman House for believing in my idea and turning it into this book.

To Kiki Loizou for writing that first piece about me in *The Sunday Times* which went on to open so many doors.

To Nigel Botterill for giving me some great marketing nuggets when I needed them!

Thanks to my friends, for simply being there for me. It doesn't matter how much you achieve in life; if you don't have people to share it all with, it is worthless.

And finally a massive, huge, huge thank you to all the amazing people who contributed to this book, it means so much to me.